Stro...   o...S.Vincenzo

icudi I. o   Filicudi I. Sal...

            Lipari I...

        Vulcano o...   ...Faro

            Milazzo o...
                        MESSINA

Cefalu   S.Agata o...   Barcellona   Str. of Messina   Reggio
                                    Ste.

Ibuono   o Mistretta

        Mt ETNA   o Taormina

    Troina o
    Nicosia   Brontes
    Agira o   o Aderno   Acireale
            Paterno o

...ini   o Castrogiovanni   CATANIA
o Caltanissetta   Gulf of
                            Catania
    Piazza o Armerina
        Caltagirone   C. Campolato

                                Augusta

            o Vizzini
            Palazzolo   Siracusa

...anova   Vittoria o Comiso
        o Ragusa   o Avola
    Modica o   o Noto
C. Scaramia   o Spaccaforno
                Pachino o   o C. Passero

OF SICILY

THINGS SEEN IN SICILY

TEMPLE OF CASTOR AND POLLUX, GIRGENTI

Where almonds bloom among the ruins and peasant children are dressed like their elders.

THINGS SEEN IN
SICILY

A DESCRIPTION OF ONE OF THE MOST BEAUTIFUL ISLANDS OF
THE WORLD WITH ITS ANCIENT BUILDINGS OF GOLDEN
SANDSTONE & ITS INTERESTING PEOPLE : A LAND
OF LEGEND & HISTORY

BY
ISABEL EMERSON

WITH ILLUSTRATIONS & SKETCH MAP

London
Seeley, Service & Co. Limited
196 Shaftesbury Avenue

Contents

List of Illustrations

List of Illustrations

List of Illustrations

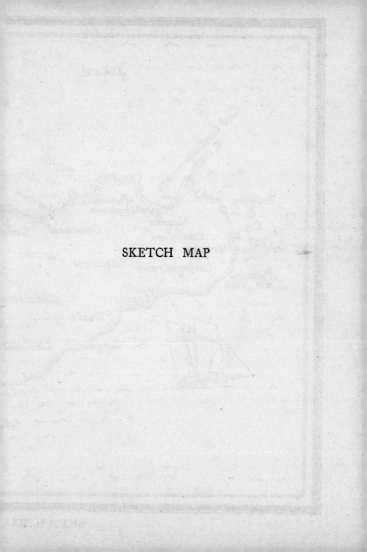

SKETCH MAP

SKETCH MAP

OF SICILY

Note for Readers who intend to Visit Sicily

The best time to visit Sicily is in the spring, though for a long stay it is enjoyable from October or November till the end of May. The summer months are hot and dry and water is scarce in many parts.

Near the coast the climate is mild all through the winter, the greatest rainfall being in November and December. The almond blossom is in its full beauty in February at Taormina and rather later elsewhere; the *zagara* or lemon blossom reaches perfection in April.

In February there are picturesque Carnival festivities in many places. In April and May classical plays are often given in the Greek theatres of Syracuse and Taormina and among the temples of Girgenti, while at Palermo there are processions of Sicilian carts and costumes, and the Madonie Circuit automobile races. April and May are the best months for visiting the interior and the Aeolian Islands.

Those who can spend only a month or so in Sicily should arrange to go in February, March or April. All through the spring months the Italian railways allow a reduction of 50 per cent. on return tickets to Sicily (Primavera Siciliana) valid for 30–40 days, from all stations in the kingdom.

Photo   Cutler

PLAYING THE CORNAMUSA OR SICILIAN BAGPIPES

The shepherd-musicians come down from their mountain villages at
Christmas to play before wayside shrines and from house to house.

Things Seen in Sicily

CHAPTER I

SICILY—GEM OF THE SOUTH

SICILY! Sicilia! What music there is in the very name of that island set like a precious jewel in the blue Mediterranean; that stepping-stone between Europe and Africa which partakes of the characteristics of both continents!

To mention Sicily is to call up a vision of green hill-sides and fertile valleys, white sands washed by indigo seas, purple mountains capped with snow, and, towering above them all, great Etna watching in pure majesty over the fair land of which she is undisputed queen.

Sicily the Enchantress, sung by poets in all ages, beloved alike by gods and men, casts her powerful spell far and wide over the earth. She is the dream, the goal, of thousands of would-be travellers, while those who have once visited her enchanted shores, carry in their hearts the ceaseless longing to return.

In what does this spell consist that its power should be felt by persons of all nationalities, and of widely differing culture and tastes? Perhaps the secret lies in the infinite variety, the manifold beauty and interest contained in an area of only about 10,000 square miles, within which each one may find what he seeks—something which makes a personal appeal to him.

The lover of Nature may feast his eyes on the ever-changing sea, rich in blue and purple hues, growing pink and then wine dark at sunset, exactly as Homer describes it in the Odyssey. Grey-brown hills rise fold upon fold above the rich green and gold of orange and lemon groves, the fairy white and blush pink of almond blossom. Near at hand, in fields and gardens, colour runs riot, blazing from hedges of scarlet geranium, bushes of hibiscus, masses of purple iris and palest mauve stock, while great dark violets of a size and perfume peculiar to Sicily, nestle at the foot of tall palms, whose luxuriant growth reminds us that Africa is not far away.

Among all the glowing colours painted by Nature's lavish brush, green and gold predominate in the Sicilian landscape. Grey-green hills, emerald-green valleys, groves of dark green trees amid whose polished foliage gleams the golden fruit and under whose shadow the ground is carpeted with pale yellow oxalis, that delicate, sweet-scented, typically Sicilian flower. Acres of feathery yellow mustard, patches of deep orange marigolds among grass-grown ruins. Temples of golden sandstone, fields of ripening corn—and in keeping with the landscape, gaily painted yellow carts file in slow procession along the winding roads. The prevailing tint is repeated even underground, for the mines of Sicily do not yield black coal like those of the grim north, but yellow sulphur, that precious product of the sunbaked earth ! And the golden sunlight sheds its blessing on this favoured land, whose mild and sunny climate caused Cicero to declare that the sun is seen at least once on every day in the year.

Among the mountains and bleak uplands of the interior cold and snow may be found ; lovers of winter sports betake themselves to the Madonie and Nebrodi mountains ; and those adventurous souls who penetrate

18

A SICILIAN ITINERANT VENDOR

Turiddu, the jar seller, hawks his wares from village to village, always
sure of a welcome and a ready sale, for the white porous clay jars keep
the water ice cool.

inland too early in the year are condemned to shiver in comfortless inns, while hurricanes of wind and rain beat on the ill-fitting windows, and the chilliness without is equalled by the chilliness of fireless rooms within. Most visitors, however, keep to the smiling country near the coast, where the hills are covered with luxuriant vegetation, the valleys with orange and lemon groves.

The curious geological formation of the island tells a tale of primeval convulsions—natural phenomena which find an echo in the myths recounted by the mariners of ancient Greece. Sicily is the home of classic myth, where every natural feature has its legendary explanation.

The smiling fertility of the land is attributed to its having been sprinkled with the blood of Uranus, slain by his son Kronos. The Titan Enceladus, chained by Zeus under the weight of Etna, shakes the mountain as he moves uneasily in his bonds and causes it to vomit smoke and molten lava in his vain efforts to free himself from his age-long torment. Those rocks in the sea near Acireale were hurled by Polyphemus the Cyclops, son of Poseidon, at the fleeing Odysseus who had blinded him. And it was at Enna, in the heart of the island, that the earth opened at the bidding of Hades to receive him and his unwilling bride Persephone. To this day the asphodel which the ill-fated maiden was gathering when the King of the Lower Regions beheld and loved her, grows tall and delicately pink on the Sicilian hills ; but it must not be gathered and carried home, for it is the flower of death, and if unwarily placed in a vase, will fill the room with the odour of corruption.

So strongly does the classical spirit brood over this land that when from the verdant hill-side a faint tinkling sylvan melody is borne to us on the breeze, we catch our

Legends

breath in an awestruck whisper: " Can it be the flute of Pan ? " For all things fantastic and mythical, all strange survivals of the world's youth, seem possible, even probable, in the dreamy Sicilian noon. . . .

The historian Tommaso Fazello, writing in the XVIth century, mentions a popular belief still current in his day, that the first corn which grew in Sicily was not sown by man but sprouted by spontaneous generation from the rich soil.

A charming legend as to the origin of the island, preserved in a quaint dialect poem, states that God created Sicily in a moment of supreme content. A diamond from the crown of the Almighty, endowed with the seven elements and flung into the southern sea, formed the nucleus round which grew the magic land. The poem concludes :

" Men call it Sicily ; but it is the diamond of the Eternal Father."

Another legend says :

" In the beginning of time Sicily was joined to the mainland, but it became detached in the universal deluge. When San Francesco di Paola wished to cross the Strait of Messina he could not find a boatman to ferry him across. So he took his cloak and, tying one corner to his staff, spread the rest on the waves and standing upon it sailed across the Strait. And all the boatmen, beholding the miracle, followed the Saint imploring him to enter their boats."

Another ancient belief is that Sicily is sustained by three columns which form the bases of her three feet ; one is under the Faro at Messina, one under Cape Passero in the south, and one under Trapani. The island was called Trinacria from these three headlands. We read in Ottley Perry's *Ranks, Badges and Dates* that " Joan,

Photo

Sport & General

THE GREEK THEATRE, TAORMINA

This magnificent theatre, built of Roman brick on a Greek foundation, looks towards Etna, with the white town of Taormina and green hills and valleys in between.

the sister of King John of England (1199–1215), married William II, King of Sicily. The three-legged badge, which first appears in the records of Mann (Isle of Man) about 1266, had previously been the badge of Sicily for 150 years."

Leaving the realms of myth and legend, few countries can boast such an eventful history as this island, separated from Italy by a narrow strait but oceans apart in the story and character of its inhabitants, who talk of crossing to the mainland as " going to the continent," and speak a dialect which other Italians often cannot understand, any more than they can understand the character of these islanders, in which violent passions and mediæval chivalry are strangely blended.

Sicily contains a greater variety of ethnical types than any similar area elsewhere can produce, for the many races who successively lived and ruled there have all left their mark on the population, a mark so indelible as to be easily recognisable in some cases at the present day. There is an obvious predominance of the Greek type in the east and south and of the Saracen and Phœnician in the north-west, while scattered here and there Norman and Spanish types may be seen. The history of the island and her many rulers is also written in unmistakable characters in the architecture of her towns.

The earliest inhabitants of Sicily, called in Greek Sikelia or Trinacria, were a prehistoric race who left their traces in the form of flint instruments and stone monuments in various parts of the island. Next came the Sicanians, whose origin is uncertain. Freeman thinks they belonged to an Iberian race of which only the Basques now survive, but other authorities believe them and the Siculians who followed them to have been two branches of an Italic race. Tradition makes them

Early History

autochthones, or sprung from the earth. Some Sicanians were still left in the west as late as the IVth century B.C.

The Siculians spoke a language akin to Latin. They are mentioned in the Odyssey and have left many remains all over the island, especially in the south-east ; about the XVth century B.C. they seem to have had commercial relations with the Mycenians and Ægeans, thus preparing the way for the Greek colonists (Dorians and Chalcidians) who came in the VIIIth and VIIth centuries, and by degrees drove them into the interior or gradually absorbed them, so that after the death in 439 of their leader Ducetius, who had made a last stand for independence, the Siculians ceased to exist as a separate people.

During all this early period the Phœnicians had numerous flourishing colonies along the coast, but at the coming of the Greeks they gradually retired to the north, to Panormos, and placed themselves under the protection of the Carthaginians, thus originating a long series of wars.

The Elymians, a mysterious race said to have come from Troy, founded Segesta, Eryx and other towns.

The long struggle between Greeks and Carthaginians, in which Gelon, Tyrant of Syracuse, was victorious and became master of the whole island in 476, was renewed by his successors, Dionysius being also victorious, but Hiero II in his siege of Messina, which was in possession of the Mamertines or Campanian mercenaries, was obliged in 274 to seek the help of the Romans ; thus the Romans came to Sicily and after the Punic Wars eventually obtained the sovereignty of the island, which became the first Roman province.

The Carthaginians had introduced an excellent agricultural system of which the Romans took full advantage, and for a time Sicily was the granary of

Introduction of Christianity

Italy; but the prosperity of the island steadily declined owing to the incessant civil wars. After the fall of the Empire it came under the power of the Ostrogoths, but in A.D. 535 the Byzantine general Belisarius conquered it for the Eastern Empire. In 827 the Saracens gained possession of the island; the Christians were driven to the north-east corner and Palermo became the capital.

There are various traditions as to the introduction of Christianity into Sicily; historical evidence points to its having been brought by missionaries from the East. It is recorded in the Acts of the Apostles that St. Paul landed at Syracuse and spent three days there on his way to Rome, but it was only after the end of the IIIrd century, in the reign of Constantine, that the new religion became general, and even in the VIth century there were still many Pagans in the island. In those early days of Christianity Sicily gave four Popes to the Church: Agathon (679), Leo II (682), Sergius (687), and Stephen (768). The bishoprics of Syracuse, Panormus, Catania, Messina, Agrigentum and Tauromenium all claim Apostolic origin.

Under Saracen rule the prosperity of the island increased, notwithstanding frequent civil wars. In 1038, Georgio Maniaces partially reconquered it for the Emperor Michael Paphlagonius. In 1060 came the Normans under Count Roger and his brother Duke Robert Guiscard, who finally, in 1096, divided the island between them. In 1130 King Roger II was crowned in Palermo cathedral, and, stern warrior though he was, art and letters flourished at his court, where Norman austerity and Saracen splendour was curiously mingled, and as a result those magnificent Norman-Arabic buildings sprang up, glittering with Byzantine mosaics.

Frederick II (1197–1250) was a precursor of modern

Later History

thought and loved to gather round him scientists and men of letters. Noteworthy among these was Ciullo d'Alcamo, the earliest of vernacular poets. Frederick himself was a writer of Italian verse and some fragments of his writings are still extant.

The Norman dynasty ended with the defeat and death at Benevento of Frederick's son Manfred, whose heroic and picturesque figure was immortalised by Dante (*Purgatorio*, Canto III). Charles of Anjou then became King of Sicily; but his bad government provoked a terrible vengeance in the massacre of the Sicilian Vespers (1282), after which Peter of Aragon was called to the throne. Under his rule the prosperity of the island decreased until it became a mere appanage of the Kingdoms of Naples and Spain. In 1713 it passed into the hands of Victor Amedeus of Savoy, who was compelled to relinquish it for Sardinia, and with Philip V (Bourbon) originated the Kingdom of the Two Sicilies.

During the Napoleonic wars Lord Nelson played a prominent part in the defence of Sicily. After various stormy vicissitudes under the Bourbon government and a year and a half of independence under Ruggiero Settimo, the Sicilians, longing for unity with Italy, impatiently awaited the hour of their redemption, which came at last in May 1860, when Garibaldi landed at Marsala with his Thousand Volunteers, and by a series of almost miraculous victories rescued the island from the oppressor; in October of the same year it became part of the Kingdom of United Italy.

This short summary of Sicilian history will show how eventful has been the life of the island from the earliest times and how the blending of many races has gone to form the Sicilians of the present day—a splendid race sprung from all that was best in their strangely mixed

Painting

ancestry. Brave, chivalrous and loyal, but at the same time jealous and revengeful, once their love is given they are faithful unto death. Even the Mafia had its origin in a political necessity and in a chivalrous effort to protect the weak against the strong, though it degenerated into common brigandage and blackmail. It has now practically ceased to exist, and travellers may venture without fear into the heart of the island, sure of meeting with that courteous treatment for which the Sicilians are famous. In 1852 there were only 750 miles of carriage roads in Sicily; now it is possible to motor all over the island.

Sicily is a happy hunting ground for the archæologist, for she is rich in prehistoric, Phœnician, Greek, Roman and early Christian remains, many of them in a wonderful state of preservation; she is said to possess more Greek temples and theatres than are to be found in the whole of Greece. Every year excavation brings to light new and priceless treasures, vases, coins and ruins of the different epochs. These discoveries follow one another with such rapidity that any remarks on the subject must necessarily soon become out of date.

In the world-wide interest and enthusiasm for these classical monuments, the mediæval art of the island is apt to be overlooked, and many persons are not even aware that Sicily possesses her own school of painting, as distinct from that of Naples.

This school came into being somewhat later than those of the mainland, for the Byzantine influence continued until the end of the XIVth century, when the first indigenous painters, Simone da Corleone and Cecco da Naro, attempted timidly to break away from Byzantine rigidity. It was only in the XVth century, however, that Sicilian painting began to hold its own.

Among several stars of lesser magnitude, Antonello

Sculpture

da Messina (1430–79) stands out as one of the great masters of the Renaissance. His art was at first inspired by the Flemish masters, later by the Venetians and Lombards, but finally his own personality emerged with strong individuality. He combines classical feeling with rich colouring and delicate sweetness of expression, while his minuteness of detail recalls the Flemish school.

In the XVIth and XVIIth centuries Caravaggio (1495–1543) and Pietro Novelli (1603–47) were shining lights, the latter rivalling Ribera in the realism of his figures, many of whom were contemporary portraits. In the XVIIIth century Giuseppe Velasquez of Palermo did fine work; he was followed in the XIXth century by Francesco Vaccaro. A group of present-day painters worthily uphold the traditions of the Sicilian School.

In the field of sculpture the earliest Sicilian master of note is Francesco Laurana (1458–1572), a Dalmatian who worked for many years in Sicily, introducing classical forms of architecture and leaving many statues whose influence acted strongly on Domenico and Antonello Gagini; examples of their work, some very beautiful, are to be found all over Sicily.

In the XVIth century came Giovanni Montorsoli (1506–93), a pupil of Michelangelo, two of whose magnificent fountains adorn the city of Messina. Giacomo Serpotta (1656–1732), brought the then popular stucco work to a high degree of perfection.

In the realm of music the island has produced several famous composers, chief among them being Alessandro Scarlatti (1659–1725) and Vincenzo Bellini (1801–35).

The Sicilians have always been adepts in goldsmith's work and their churches and museums are rich in sacred vessels of great artistic beauty. Their majolica is very interesting and their lace and embroidery are well known.

CHAPTER II

SARACEN AND NORMAN SICILY : PALERMO

A WIDE and glorious bay bounded by two rugged headlands rising abruptly from the plain; a fair city cradled between them and stretching inland towards a background of sheltering mountains; broad, clean streets behind whose geometrical precision lies a network of teeming, crooked, clothes-hung alleys; a vision of tall palms, their feathery crests softly stirring in the sea breeze, which carries the scent of lemon blossom far out over the waters of the great bay; all these greet the traveller as he gazes entranced at the white city gleaming in the morning light and framed in the green and gold of the Conca d' Oro.

This is Palermo, La Felice, the City of Palm Trees, whose primitive name, given by the first Phœnician settlers, was Tsits, a flower. The Greeks called it Panormos—all harbour—for its harbour was formerly much larger than it is at present.

Panormos was an important Carthaginian stronghold until the Romans conquered it in 254 B.C. Hamilcar Barca besieged it for three years from the heights of Monte Pellegrino but was unable to recapture it. In A.D. 535 Belisarius took it from the Ostrogoths and it remained under the Byzantine Emperors until the Saracens came in 827 and made it their prosperous capital. It was then ruled by the Normans, the Suabians and Charles of Anjou, until the latter was expelled after the massacre of the Sicilian Vespers in 1282. Later the

Architecture

Spanish Viceroys chose Palermo as their residence and it once more became a gay and fashionable capital. The Neapolitan court twice took refuge there and Ferdinand I lived there until 1815. The Sicilian parliament met there in 1812. Between 1820 and 1860 the city fell on evil days, being twice bombarded in times of revolt, and losing many inhabitants in an outbreak of cholera. It was finally stormed by Garibaldi, who entered in triumph on May 27th, 1860.

Of the many races who have dominated Palermo each has left some trace in the architecture of the city, a fact which must be borne in mind in seeking to understand the bewildering and picturesque variety of styles presented by churches and palaces. The Norman and Saracen influences predominate and are often found strangely blended, as in the Royal Palace, which was built by the Saracens as a fortress, and added to by the Normans. These built the central tower, Santa Ninfa, while that gem the Cappella Palatina was built by King Roger II in Arabic-Norman style, and enriched with Byzantine mosaics which recall the jewelled fire of the Ravenna churches, though it is more warmly Oriental than they, owing to the play of light and shade through narrow windows, and the mystery of Saracen arches supporting a painted wooden ceiling of stalactite design. A small room said to have been decorated for Roger is also rich in mosaics. This partiality for glowing, glittering, Eastern colours, noticeable also in Cefalù cathedral, founded by him and possessing the oldest mosaics in Sicily, throws an interesting sidelight on the character and tastes of the Norman warrior-king.

Another example of this curious blending of styles is found in the cathedral, built between 1169 and 1185 by the English Archbishop Gualtiero Offamilio (Walter of

Photo   *D'Agata*

MOUNT ETNA FROM TAORMINA

Etna's white majesty masks hidden fires and limitless powers of destruction.
The ex-monastery of San Domenico is seen perched on the cliff edge.

San Giovanni degli Eremiti

the Mill) on the site of an ancient church which had been converted into a mosque and then re-consecrated. The symmetry of this building has been spoiled by the ill-judged addition of a heavy dome, but on the east side much of the ancient character is preserved and the west façade and south door are very fine. In this church stand the Tombs of the Kings ; six massive porphyry sarcophagi containing the remains of Roger and his successors ; these tombs were originally in the cathedral of Cefalù.

The most picturesque of all the Palermo churches is San Giovanni degli Eremiti, which, with its five red domes, has the outward appearance of a mosque; it was in fact adapted from one in 1132 and the remains of this are still to be seen on the south side. The charming flower-grown cloisters are the haunt of artists. It was the bell of this church which gave the signal for the massacre of the Sicilian Vespers.

I remember on a first visit to Palermo in 1903 being greatly amused by the old custodian of this church, who, in order to explain its history to the foreign visitors, helped out his limited English vocabulary with a vivid pantomime of the great massacre.

" Ding ! Ding ! Ding ! " he cried, pointing to the tower and pulling an imaginary bell-rope ; then drew a finger backwards and forwards across his throat with a gruesome and realistic gurgle !

That cheery old man is no longer at his post in the church he used to show with such pride, and with his passing some of the quaint charm of San Giovanni degli Eremiti has vanished.

On a recent visit I was told that during Lent, in memory of the Sicilian Vespers, the Palermo church bells are beaten with hammers instead of being rung in the ordinary way. Whether this is a fact I cannot say, but I certainly saw some boys in the belfry of a church adjoining San Giovanni, hammering merrily on the bells, and was nearly deafened by the metallic clangour thus produced !

Within an enclosure reached by a flight of steps near the Quattro Canti or central point of the city, are two churches of about the same date ; San Cataldo with a Saracenic battlemented frieze and three domes, the central one supported by four columns ; and La Martorana or Santa Maria dell' Ammiraglio, a fine Byzantine basilica built by Giorgios Antiochenos, an admiral of Roger II. Of the mosaics which originally adorned this church only two remain, badly restored ; one of these represents Giorgios Antiochenos crouching in a quaint tortoise-like attitude at the feet of the Virgin ; the other shows King Roger being crowned by Christ. (Not by the Pope, of whom he got the better in a long struggle for supremacy !) A similar mosaic at Monreale shows King William the Good being crowned by Christ ; in another he offers a model of the church to the Madonna.

Outside the Porta Nuova, a fine gateway adjoining the Royal palace and built in 1535 to record Charles V's entry into Palermo on his return from Tunis, are the remains of two palaces, La Cuba and La Zisa, built by Saracen architects for the Norman kings, and more wholly Arabic in feeling and design than any other buildings in Palermo. An old legend accounts for them thus :

" Once upon a time there was in Palermo a Saracen king who had two daughters beautiful as the morning and loved by him with a jealous affection. Seeing that he was old and that the time drew near when Allah would call him to the delights of the black-eyed houris in

ON THE QUAY AT PALERMO

The characteristic Sicilian carts, painted with incidents from the Tales of Chivalry, are waiting to be loaded with merchandise. Monte Pellegrino guards the entrance to the harbour.

La Zisa & La Cuba

Paradise, he wished to leave to each of his daughters a palace where she should reign as queen. So he summoned architects and builders, workers in marble and mosaic, and commanded them to build two palaces in the plain beyond the city, one here and one there in a great park which stretched from north to south as far as the mountains. And two marvellous palaces arose, surrounded by gardens and fishponds.

"The king was gathered to his fathers and when the princesses had mourned him with all due rites they withdrew each to her palace. The elder, Aziza, took the larger; the younger, Cuba, dwelt in the smaller, which was not less beautiful than the other. And in process of time they also died, leaving their names to the two palaces."

This legend was still current in the XVth century, but later the Arabic inscriptions on the walls of the two buildings were deciphered and proved that La Zisa (Arabic *aziz*, splendid) was built by William the Bad, and La Cuba (*cuba*, a dome) by his son William the Good.

La Cuba, which is mentioned by Boccaccio (*Decameron*, VIth Tale of Vth Day), has been used as barracks and allowed to fall into a sad state of ruin, but is now being restored and lovely bits of stalactite work have been discovered and cleaned. In a lemon orchard which once formed part of the grounds of La Cuba stands La Cubola, an exquisite little pavilion with red dome and pointed arches, so completely Arabic that standing before it one is transported in thought to Tunis with its mosques and Marabout tombs.

La Zisa is a high square building whose central hall or court remains intact with its stalactite decoration, its running water and arch ornamented with devils which, according to a popular superstition, cannot be counted, the number never working out twice the same, though they are said to be thirteen.

The palaces belonging to the period of Spanish occupation may be recognised by the bulging shape and elaborate decoration of their iron and stone balconies, said to have been designed for the convenience of fashionable ladies of the period in their hooped skirts.

Most of the Palermo churches are in baroque (XVIIth century) style, San Domenico being a fine example owing to its spaciousness. It is an imposing building standing back from the Via Roma in a *piazza* shaded by palm-trees, and contains the tombs or monuments of many famous Palermitans, among them the painter Pietro Novelli, the historian Amari, Francesco Crispi the statesman, Ruggiero Settimo, who assembled the Sicilian parliament in this church in 1848, and Pitrè, author of a number of books on Sicilian customs and folklore and founder of the interesting Ethnological Museum in the Via Maqueda. A tablet in the south aisle bears the following inscription :

A NINA—ORNAMENTO DEL SICOLO PARNASO

> Cara alle grazie a poetar fu prima
> Tra il vago sesso nel volgare in rima
> Astro d' amor brillò nel ciel Sicano
> Per fama accese Dante da Maiano.

Fiorì nel secolo di Federico lo Svevo verso il MCCLXXX.

(TO NINA—ORNAMENT OF THE SICILIAN PARNASSUS

> Dear to the graces was her name who sung
> First of the gentle sex in vulgar tongue.
> Her star shone bright in the Sicilian sky
> Kindling the torch by Dante held on high.

She flourished in the century of Frederick the Suabian about MCCLXXX.)

SAN GIOVANNI DEGLI EREMITI, PALERMO

From the tower of this church, once a mosque, the signal was given for
the massacre of the Sicilian Vespers

Gardens

One would like to know more of the fair poetess who at so early a date followed in the footsteps of Ciullo d' Alcamo !

San Giuseppe at the Quattro Canti is interesting in that it consists of an upper and a lower church, the latter much frequented and having a crypt. But far more graceful is the XVth-century Santa Maria della Catena, near the Marina ; this church takes its name from the chain which was formerly stretched across the harbour. Close by are the Porta Felice (1644) and several buildings with low massive square arches of Egyptian style. Certainly variety is not wanting in the architecture of Palermo !

And what infinite variety in the street scenes of this fascinating city, where scent and colour mingle in Oriental profusion and where one feels nearer to the East than in any other Sicilian town ! This illusion is partly due to the presence of palms and other tropical trees, but also to something indefinably Oriental in the inhabitants. Palms are everywhere, growing tall and straight, small green oases amid the bustle of the busy streets. Eight of them in a semicircle mount guard over a fountain where a seahorse, green with moss, prances above the splashing water. A row of them guards the approach to the church of San Domenico. Their tall heads appear over the high walls of private gardens even in the heart of the city. And they reach their apotheosis in the Giardino Bonanno, opposite the Royal Palace, where no other tree breaks the harmony of their slim stems and feathery crests and where they rise out of carefully tended flower-beds, bright even in winter with roses, stocks, ageratum and all manner of summer blossoms.

Palermo is rich in public gardens. There is the large and symmetrically perfect Villa Giulia, the Orto Botanico,

C

Streets

wilder and more picturesque, the Giardino Inglese, La Favorita, that great park at the foot of Monte Pellegrino. And smaller than any of these, but perhaps more attractive, the Giardino Garibaldi invites the wayfarer to stray among shady paths and seats, glowing scarlet hibiscus and marvellous tropical trees. There the gigantic *Ficus Magnolia* with its broad and shiny leaves flings down from its branches long tresses which reach the ground and, taking root, form new trunks around the parent trunk, so that in time one tree will become a forest. Then there is the *Ficus Beniamina*, a small-leaved tree which follows the same habit, twisting its many trunks together till they look like a mass of serpents. Anything less like the common fig-tree than these two tropical marvels would be difficult to imagine, but the connecting link consists in the small, undeveloped fruit of both, which on close examination is found to resemble a tiny fig.

Seen from the height of Monreale, Palermo shows a ground plan amazing in its rectilinear precision. The Corso Vittorio Emanuele, originally named Cassaro from *El Kars*, the castle, and called Corso Calatafimi outside the Porta Nuova, leads in one unbroken line from La Rocca to the sea. The Via Maqueda, equally straight, crosses it at the Quattro Canti and is prolonged beyond the Teatro Massimo and the Politeama Garibaldi, two imposing theatres standing each in a fine *piazza*, and becomes the Via della Libertà, a new and spacious avenue flanked by handsome palaces and gardens, of which the Palermitans are justly proud. Nearer the sea the Corso is crossed by the Via Roma, another well-laid-out main street.

Except for the colour and perfume and the ubiquitous palms, these streets might belong to any European

Photo   *Underwood Press Service*

GOATS MILKED WHILE YOU WAIT

In Old Palermo the milkman leads his flock from door to door, holding up
the traffic while he serves his customers.

Local Customs

capital. The true and characteristic Palermo lies between and behind them, but so close behind that a step takes one over the threshold into another world; the teeming labyrinth of the Old Town, which is not a separate quarter, it is everywhere. The wide and handsome streets have been ruthlessly cut through it and their tall buildings act as a screen for its picturesque squalor.

Descend that flight of steps from the Via Maqueda and you are in the market. And what a market! A central square surrounded by crooked houses and the openings of innumerable alleys, all crowded with stalls. Stalls and shops are everywhere. Food of all kinds is heaped up in reckless profusion. Here as everywhere gold and green predominate; golden oranges, green vegetables. Close by are fish of every size, shape and hue, and meat in large quantities. Here an open door framed in primitive and highly-coloured posters leads to a Marionette Theatre; there, under the sign *Trattoria* (eating house) stands mine host, stout and friendly, welcoming his customers with promises of *pasta con sarde*, macaroni with fish sauce; while within the low room his numerous progeny scream and tumble among the tables and his wife is seen through an opening in the partition, preparing this extraordinary mixture over a charcoal fire.

The shoppers in the market are chiefly men, for Palermitan women, except the very poorest, do not go out for household shopping as in Rome or Florence. In houses where no servant is kept the husband buys the day's provisions before going to his work. His wife stays at home in almost Oriental seclusion, only going out to attend Mass or take the children to school, never to shop or carry parcels. In the evening or on Sunday her husband will occasionally take her out on his arm for a mild

The Smaller Streets

walk. Sicilian women are naturally indolent mentally and physically and their evolution is centuries behind that of the men, who do not find or expect intellectual companionship in their homes. Their attitude to their wives is one of protective, jealous ownership mingled with a chivalrous respect for women ; they are generally good husbands and bear the whole weight of the household responsibilities.

One one occasion, being the only woman in a crowded railway carriage between Cefalù and Palermo, I overheard a discussion between a good-looking Palermitan of Saracen type and a much-travelled acquaintance, evidently of Norman ancestry, as to the best way to treat their wives. The dialogue was worthy of Aristophanes and might have stood for the Two Logics of East and West.

The Saracen maintained that the only way to keep a wife faithful is to shut her up, as women only need opportunity to go astray. The Norman was in favour of more humane methods of trust and sympathy, saying that if a woman goes astray it is usually in search of the affection and understanding often denied her by her husband, who by means of loving comprehension could make her all that he desires.

Most of the men present sided with the Saracen, whose view is still the more generally accepted in Sicily ; they evidently thought the other a visionary crank. They all spoke with absolute unreserve and abundance of detail, little dreaming that the *forestiera* sitting silent in the corner could understand their discussion. It was an interesting sidelight on Sicilian mentality !

The smaller streets in Palermo form a remarkable contrast to the principal ones we have mentioned, so winding and tortuous are they. If in a hurry it is fatal

The Smaller Streets

to plunge into these *vicoli*, which twist and turn so unaccountably that it is difficult to keep one's bearings, and there is more probability of emerging near the starting-point than of arriving at the desired destination.

Crowded together in picturesque confusion are buildings of every period ; among the squalid dwellings of the very poor a mediæval palace rears its magnificent façade, the lofty doorway framing a view of pillared courtyard, and the stone or iron balconies showing the date of building. Some of these slums are not overclean and one has to pick one's way among decaying vegetables and other rubbish, for everything is flung into the street, sometimes from upper windows, with disastrous consequences for passers by ! But beggars are rare and the natural courtesy or Oriental indifference of the Palermitans prevents undue staring at the stranger. If by chance a few urchins do gather round, there is always someone ready to send them about their business with an admonitory " *jammuninn' !* " (get along !)

In the main streets the names over the shops are curious and savour of mythical monsters and mediæval paladins : Quattrocchi (Four eyes), Cinquemani (Five hands), Ruggero, Orlando, etc. ; as to the wares displayed in the confectioners' windows, their variety and originality baffle description. Long before Mid-Lent Easter Eggs and Paschal Lambs appear, while in the second half of March rich-looking buns filled with a creamy, spicy mixture and rejoicing in the name *Sfinge di San Giuseppe* are on sale. And there is always the *cassata*, sometimes a complicated ice and sometimes merely an iced cake, and the delicious *cannolo*, a crisp tube of brown pastry resembling the bark of a tree and filled with the said spicy cream.

The newcomer is struck by a rather touching custom

Carro Siciliano

which gives the idea that the death-rate among Palermitan tradesmen must be unusually high, for so many shops have a strip of black cloth stretched across the window with a card bearing the inscription : *Per mia moglie* (for my wife), *Per mia suocera* (for my mother-in-law), *Per il nostro Signor Egidio*, and so forth. But one does not see a corresponding number of persons in mourning about the streets. What one does see and wonder at is the number of able-bodied men walking about with fringed travelling rugs over their shoulders, even on warm days ! This is a curious survival of the Arab burnous or the Spanish cloak. The women, of course, wear shawls, those of Paisley pattern in bright colours being in high favour.

But perhaps the most distinctive feature in the colour scheme of Palermo is the Sicilian cart, which may be seen here in all its glory. A box-like vehicle mounted on two wheels and painted yellow, its sides are decorated with panels illustrating the warlike deeds of the paladins, Bible stories or classical legends, and its under parts and shafts are elaborately carved with heads, arabesques, sirens, etc. This cart, which is probably of Byzantine origin (we remember seeing something similar though far less elaborate in the country near Ravenna), is drawn by a horse or mule whose scarlet trappings are studded with tiny mirrors to avert the Evil Eye. Over his head nods a crimson plume ; another like a small tree surmounts the harness on his back. In the cart are often a number of peasants seated on chairs or benches and wrapped in shawls. On a *festa* one may see really lovely girls dressed in bright colours who come in from the country, where every carter's ambition is to possess a more richly painted cart than his neighbour.

The Museum

As we stand watching the varied procession of carts and carriages, all filled to overflowing—whole families out for a jaunt, or lumbering old vehicles heavy with the solid bulk of seven full-grown men—a tiny donkey trots by drawing a miniature painted cart. The gay, well-groomed little beast, no larger than a good-sized dog, shakes its beplumed head and seems quite unconcerned at the weight it is drawing : a stout man perched on sacks of coal ! In fact, all the animals here seem remarkably strong and willing ; they are evidently well fed and kindly treated, except in the matter of overloading, and respond cheerfully to the demands made on them.

There is a faint, indefinite perfume in the air of Palermo, a delicate mingling of freesia and violet, which grows stronger as one approaches the street corners ; and there they are, freesias and violets in great bouquets mounted on sticks and composed of a number of smaller bunches symmetrically arranged on twigs, to be broken off and sold separately. This is in winter and spring ; later in the year the heady perfume of the *zagara* or lemon blossom overpowers all and is wafted far out to sea.

And over all the motley, teeming life of the Sicilian capital the glorious southern sun pours down his health-giving rays.

The National Museum in the Via Roma is a treasure-house of interest. The two courts are full of sculpture and there are many fine statues and vases. Especially interesting are a perfect pavement of Roman mosaic, discovered in 1869 in the Piazza Vittoria, two Phœnician sarcophagi whose massive bulk bears a primitive resemblance to the human form, with head and hands, and the celebrated Metopes from Selinunte. On the second floor is a picture gallery containing many examples of the

San Giovanni dei Lebbrosi

Sicilian school of painting, which merits more attention than it usually receives, and a lovely little triptych of the early Flemish school.

In a room on the first floor are some life-sized stucco groups by Serpotta (1656–1732), who brought the art of modelling to such perfection that one can only regret the unresponsive lifelessness of the material in which he expressed himself.

Just outside the city, near the Oreto river, but no longer spanning it, is the Ponte dell' Ammiraglio, built in 1113 by the admiral Giorgios Antiochenos. It has eleven arches and is a fine example of pure Norman architecture, besides being the oldest existing stone bridge built since the fall of the Roman Empire.

The Oreto river was the scene of several important battles. In 251 B.C. the Roman Consul Metellus defeated the Carthaginians there and captured 120 elephants. In A.D. 1038 Giorgio Maniaces defeated the Saracens at the same spot. In 1670 the French admiral Duquesne destroyed the Dutch and Spanish fleets in the neighbouring bay. And on May 27th, 1860, Garibaldi, descending from the mountains to storm Palermo, had his first encounter with the Bourbon troops on this bridge.

At a short distince from the Ponte dell' Ammiraglio a gateway leads, through a dirty and malodorous tanyard, to the church of San Giovanni dei Lebbrosi, founded by Count Roger in 1071 and probably the oldest Norman church in Sicily. It has been restored but still preserves its original form, a small basilica with three naves. The three apses and cupola are the oldest part and are severely pure, their only ornamentation being a few delicate columns with graceful capitals built into the wall and evidently belonging to a much earlier building. The church is a little gem and certain horrible wax

The Catacombs

figures and wooden shrines strike a discordant note in this austere place of worship, which seems to bring us in touch with the stern and simple faith of the Great Count.

Nearly opposite the entrance to San Giovanni is a factory of Sicilian carts ; we enter by the open door and watch one artist carving the elaborate decoration while another paints the panels with scenes of chivalry in brilliant colours ; fortunately this traditional art is still full of vitality.

Visitors to Palermo can hardly avoid being taken to see the Catacombs of the Cappuccini, which are considered by Palermitans as one of the principal sights of their city. Guides and cab-drivers feel that their task is not accomplished until they have deposited their charges before the white portico of the monastery, in whose subterranean chambers are preserved the bodies of some eight thousand rich citizens. These gruesome relics, some mummified, others skeletons, all fully clothed in the dress of their day, sit, stand or recline along the corridors. This mode of burial was in vogue until 1881, when it was forbidden by the Government. The spectacle is anything but pleasing and its hair-raising qualities are enhanced by the occasional movement of a skull, caused by the scramblings of a mouse within ; but its strangeness appeals to the curious.

It is a question whether more courage be required to visit this gloomy museum of death or to refuse to do so, for if one replies in the negative to the inevitable : " Have you been to the Cappuccini ? " an expression of pained surprise dawns on the questioner's face and he continues in a tone of persuasive remonstrance :

" But it is most interesting—*interessantissimo*—you must not leave Palermo without going there ! "

The Catacombs

And the advice is often accompanied by an offer of escort.

Should you persist in your refusal, fate and the southern sun seem to fight against your obstinacy. One morning you set out on foot to visit La Zisa and lose your way among the dusty streets outside the Porta Nuova, plunging into a labyrinth of alleys whose low, white-washed dwellings recall the suburbs of Tunis and end in winding lanes between glaring white walls.

"All this is pure Saracen," you say to yourself, "I must be near La Zisa!"

At length, footsore and weary, at about midday, you emerge in an open grass-grown space before a white portico of indefinite period, where several carriages are waiting.

"What is that building?" you ask of a group of decrepit old men who hobble out of a lane leading to the back of the edifice.

"Il Convento dei Cappuccini!" they reply in the grateful tones of those who have partaken of the monk's soup. . . .

And there you are after all—too tired to walk another step and tempted by the thought of cool cloisters beyond that hospitable portal!

CHAPTER III

WHEN going by tram to Monreale—and no matter how short be the time at our disposal in Palermo, this expedition should not be omitted—we change at the station of Rocca into a kind of funicular for the steep ascent. An amusing incident witnessed here by the present writer shows that the Sicilian tram-conductor is not far behind his colleague of the London bus in those witty sallies which, though often at the expense of his passengers, are so good-humoured that they seldom give offence.

Arrived at Rocca on this particular occasion, several English and Americans sprang out quickly and secured good seats in the other car, but two or three were blocked by the slow and ponderous descent of two stout Sicilian women, not old, but evidently unaccustomed to movement. So long did they take to lower themselves heavily to the ground that the conductor, losing patience, cried :

" *Jammuninn' ! Jammuninn' !* (Hurry up !) Aren't you ashamed ? See how active these *forestiere* are, while you *Palermitane* are like so many snails ! "

The " snails " continued their stolid progress quite unmoved by this scathing remark, while those of the *forestiere* who understood were convulsed with laughter at the aptness of the simile !

The great mosaic-encrusted cathedral of Monreale is one of the marvels of Sicily and Europe. It stands in a commanding position high above the Conca d' Oro, and

43

Monreale

Palermo lies spread out like a map below, bounded by Monte Pellegrino and the sea.

In this superb situation a monastery was founded in the VIth century by Pope Gregory the Great, and later a Saracen village grew up on the spot. Here King Roger built a palace on the outskirts of the large royal park which stretched to the south and south-west of Palermo. The palace was turned into a fortress by William the Bad, and in 1166 his son, William the Good, restored it as a monastery and placed there a hundred Benedictine monks from La Cava, building close by the glorious basilica where both he and his father are buried.

A legend narrates that the King, tired with hunting, fell asleep under a tree and saw in a dream the Madonna, who revealed to him the spot where a treasure was buried, and ordered him to use it for building " the most beautiful church which art and faith combined could offer to God." And so, in a remarkably short time, the great cathedral arose, and to its building contributed Saracen, Byzantine, Sicilian and Norman artists, thus producing that marvellous blending of styles and richness of decoration which render it so beautiful and unique— an eloquent expression of the devotion of those early warrior kings, in whose tastes Northern severity and Oriental magnificence were strangely mingled.

King William dedicated his church as a votive offering for the repose of his father's bloodstained soul, and also in the hope, alas never realised, that his wife, English Joan, might bear him a son.

Before entering the church we walk round the east end and admire the triple apse ornamented with exquisite pointed and interlaced arches, whose lava and limestone decoration is most effective. This marvellous piece of architecture has remained intact since 1176. The same decoration is repeated on the west façade, where the triple portal is flanked by two massive towers of unequal height, one of them having been left unfinished or partially destroyed. The beautiful central doorway is rich in bas-relief and mosaic ; the bronze door, made by Bonanno of Pisa in 1186, has Biblical scenes in its forty-two compartments. The bronze door on the north side, by Barisano da Trani, is a fine example of XVIth-century work, but is not in keeping with the rest of the building.

We enter the church and stand bewildered by the glow and glitter that surround us. On every hand are polished marble, warmly coloured mosaics on a gold ground, graceful columns with Corinthian capitals—a wealth of lavish decoration. The detail is less remarkable than in the Cappella Palatina, the atmosphere less Oriental, but the general effect is magnificent and impressive. The basilica has three naves supported by columns, and on their walls the whole history of Old and New Testament is depicted in mosaic. Majestically dominating the central apse is an immense half-length figure of Christ, with right hand raised in blessing ; underneath are the Madonna and Child with attendant saints and angels. St. Peter and St. Paul preside over the lateral apses, decorated with scenes from their lives. The ceilings of painted wood were restored after a disastrous fire in 1811.

The XIIth-century cloisters are the finest in existence ; their delicate pairs of columns show a variety of designs and were originally encrusted with mosaic. The capitals form an interesting study, their designs varying from acanthus leaves and climbing plants to mythical monsters, heads of Demeter and Persephone, hunting scenes, Adoration of the Magi, etc. ; while on one

Il Castellaccio

capital King William offers a model of the church to the Madonna, an incident also shown in one of the mosaics.

On the staircase of the old monastery is the masterpiece of Pietro Novelli, who was a native of Monreale. This canvas represents St. Benedict giving the Rule of the Order, in the form of bread, to his assembled followers. The knight standing under the tree is a portrait of the artist and most of the figures in the picture are portraits of well-known men of his day. Another canvas by Giuseppe Velasquez of Palermo has for its subject the legend of King William and the treasure.

The garden beyond the cloisters is luxuriant with flowers ; from its wall we have a magnificent view of the Conca d' Oro with Parco on the opposite hill and the sea away to the left.

Ten minutes' walk up a rough path brings us to the small church of the Madonna delle Croci, a curious two-storeyed building of brown sandstone, whose upper portico is supported by square, Egyptian-looking arches. It clings to the rocky, flower-starred hill-side and has much of the character of an ancient temple. The view from this height is finer and more extensive than from Monreale itself.

A longer walk brings us to Il Castellaccio on the summit of Monte Caputo, an interesting Norman ruin, fortress or fortified monastery, perhaps a convalescent home for the monks of Monreale. In the same excursion may be included the monastery of San Martino delle Scale, one of the six religious houses founded in Sicily by Pope Hildebrand. It was destroyed by the Saracens, rebuilt in the XIVth century, a new church added in the XVIth century, with other additions and restorations, so that it is difficult to distinguish anything of the original

Photo   *Sport & General*

TORRE CALDURA NEAR CEFALU

There are many of these ruined watch towers, reminiscent of Saracen days, all along the coast of Sicily.

building. The church contains several fine paintings and the refectory has a fresco by Pietro Novelli.

From the valley of San Martino we may descend alongside a torrent to the picturesque hamlet of Boccadifalco, the roar of whose mills is heard from afar, and Baida, once a Saracen village, whose monastery and church were founded towards the end of the XIVth century by Manfredi Chiaramonte, lord of the surrounding lands. Boccadifalco is a good starting-point for the ascent of Monte Cuccio.

Outside the Porta Sant' Antonino, on the lower slopes of Monte Grifone, is the church of Santa Maria di Gesù, with its charming cloisters and small cemetery fragrant with flowers. The church was built in 1429 and commands a fine view of Palermo and Monte Pellegrino, the mountain which Goethe considered " the most beautiful in the world ! "

The ascent of Monte Pellegrino, never very difficult, is now made easy for all by a good carriage road to the summit. This mountain, where Hamilcar Barca had his camp in the First Punic War, became famous in later times as the retreat of Santa Rosalia, daughter of Duke Sinibaldo, who fled from the temptations of court life and lived for many years in a grotto near the summit until her death in 1166. In 1624 her bones were taken to Palermo and the plague raging in the city immediately ceased. She was then made Patroness of Palermo, and her grotto became a church much frequented by pilgrims, especially on the 4th of September. The statue of the Saint with head and hands of marble is clad in a golden robe given by Charles III. Another colossal statue standing on a rocky height above the sea has twice been decapitated by lightning.

Extending over a large area at the foot of Monte

Piana dei Greci

Pellegrino is the fine park of La Favorita, with gardens, woods and orange groves ; it belonged to the Bourbon King Ferdinand and is now thrown open to the public.

An interesting half-day excursion from Palermo is to Piana dei Greci, an Albanian village up in the hills to the left of the Conca d' Oro. The road winds upwards, the fair valley below glowing green and gold as we survey it from this height, with Monreale on the opposite hill. Through the narrow, ill-paved streets of Parco progress is necessarily slow and gives time to observe the life of the place, where pigs, hens and ragged children tumble over each other in picturesque confusion, and share the hospitality of the poor one-roomed houses. Pigs are evidently in high favour here and attain large proportions ; they may even be seen chained outside the doors like watch-dogs !

The road now enters a wild mountain pass and then descends to Piana dei Greci, whose long street opens on to a green upland valley, at the far end of which is the new reservoir. The power-station in connection with it supplies Palermo with electricity. The inhabitants of this village are the descendants of an Albanian colony founded in 1488. Several of these colonies came to Sicily, chiefly to the province of Palermo, after the death of the Albanian national hero, Scanderbeg. The people lead a life apart and do not intermarry with the Sicilians. They speak the Albanian language and belong to the Orthodox Church. The women wear something approaching a national costume, consisting of a long, dark skirt and brightly-coloured velvet bodice opening to show a snowy chemisette. They have peculiar christening and marriage ceremonies and special festivals of their own.

Leaving Palermo by the Villa Giulia, an hour's run

Photo   *Ballance*

THE CLOISTERS, MONREALE

These XIIth century cloisters are the finest in existence. Their graceful columns show a variety of designs and their capitals are rich in delicate carving.

Cefalù

over roads so bad that it would be less fatiguing to go by train, brings us to Solunto. Here we soon see a red house bearing the legend "Antichità di Solunto," and passing through a gate, find ourselves in a lemon orchard, where the custodian is waiting under the trees to conduct us up the stony hill-side to the interesting ruins. After a time we come to an ancient terra-cotta paved road and the climb becomes easier ; in all it takes about half an hour.

Solocis or Solus was one of the earliest Phœnician settlements in Sicily. After being allied to the Carthaginians it joined the Romans at the time of the First Punic War, and they rebuilt and enriched it. The paving of the streets is almost intact ; there are the remains of many houses, cisterns and ovens. A group of fluted Doric columns is thought to have belonged to the Gymnasium, and there are several well-preserved mosaic pavements.

From the top of the hill a fine view of the coast is obtained as far as Cefalù, with Sólanto, whose name is a corruption of Solunto, and Santa Flavia with its tunny fishery, lying along the shore. On the other hand we see Palermo with Cape Zafferano and Monte Pellegrino.

It seems certain that further excavation on the hill-top will bring to light the theatre which in all these towns occupied a commanding position.

Following the road which passes for miles between luxuriant lemon groves and over long bridges spanning *fiumari* or dry river-beds, we come in two or three hours to Cefalù, the ancient Cephaloedium of Sicanian or Phœnician foundation, nestling under a beetling crag, on whose summit are the remains of a mediæval castle, a Saracen cistern and fragments of an archaic building which goes by the name of Temple of Diana.

The Story of a Vow

The chief interest of Cefalù centres in its marvellous cathedral, one of the finest examples of Norman-Arabic architecture and containing the oldest mosaics in Sicily. To explain the presence of so lordly a temple in a small fishing town (for Cefalù has never been much more than this), legend relates that King Roger, when returning in 1129 from the mainland, was overtaken by a storm off the Sicilian coast. Being threatened with shipwreck he made a vow to build a church to the Saviour at the point where he should come safe to land. His ship was borne by the waves into the sheltered bay of Cefalù. His coronation and affairs of state delayed the fulfilment of this vow, but Roger did not forget ; on the day of Pentecost, 1131, he laid the foundation-stone of the great cathedral and dedicated it to San Salvatore, on the site of a Pagan temple which the Saracens had converted into a mosque.

Roger spared no expense in the building and decoration of his church ; the most skilful Saracen and Norman architects were entrusted with the work and Byzantine artists were summoned to decorate the interior with mosaic. It was completed in 1148, about forty years before the mosaics of Monreale were executed.

A flight of steps leads from the Piazza to the platform in front of the church ; the handsome iron railing is surmounted by four statues of bishops. The façade is very uncommon ; three arches, the central one round, the others pointed, support a double tier of arcades, the lower interlaced. This beautiful façade is flanked by two tall towers. A colonnade of interlaced arches runs round the cornice of transept and apse. It is altogether a most imposing building and the interior does not disappoint the expectations raised by the magnificent exterior.

Photo   Alinari

THE FACADE OF THE CATHEDRAL, CEFALU

This fine example of Norman-Arabic architecture was built by King Roger in the XIIth century
and contains the oldest mosaics in Sicily.

The Story of a Vow

We enter a basilica with three naves, whose arches rest on granite columns. The raftered roof shows traces of gilding and inscriptions ; the name Manfredi and the date 1263 are still legible. There are several tombs and a XIIth-century black marble font. On the last column on the left is a curious painted figure commonly called " Re Ruggero," which has a certain resemblance to the mosaic portrait of the Empress Theodora in San Vitale at Ravenna.

From the moment of entering the church our attention is held by the great mosaic in the apse—a colossal half-figure of Christ, the right hand raised in blessing, the left holding a book. While similar to that at Monreale, this older mosaic in plainer surroundings is far more impressive. The eyes seem to follow us everywhere with a stern and majestic glance. This is truly Christ the King.

Below the great central Figure is the Madonna, with angels, apostles, prophets and saints ; on the vaulting above float hosts of cherubim and seraphim—all in glowing mosaic, whose gold, red and blue blend with Oriental richness and form a glittering firmament out of which the great Christ head looks, as though surveying and gravely blessing the world.

The graceful cloisters with their double columns and carved capitals recall those of Monreale, though one side has been spoiled by injudicious restoration.

A mantle of gold brocade said to have been worn by King Roger at the laying of the foundation-stone is preserved in the sacristy.

CHAPTER IV

SARACEN AND NORMAN SICILY : TRAPANI AND MONTE
SAN GIULIANO

IF we approach Trapani by sea our first impression
is of a white city stretching along the shore and
crowned by green-tiled cupolas. The ancient towers of
Ligny and Colombaia guard the entrance to the harbour,
and a broad, tree-planted esplanade runs along the
water's edge.

The journey from Palermo occupies a few hours
either by sea or railway. The line does not follow the
coast but turns inland after Castellamare del Golfo,
once the port of Segesta, and passing through Alcamo,
Calatafimi and Castelvetrano (the station for Selinunte),
proceeds up the west coast by Mazzara and Marsala and
so to Trapani.

It is quicker and more convenient to go by road, for
a motor-bus called the *direttissimo* performs the journey
in less time, and a very interesting journey it is.

Skirting the base of Monte Pellegrino we pass through
Mondello, the favourite bathing resort of the Palermitans ; then through several small towns whose
strangely Oriental appearance reminds us that we are
still in Saracen Sicily. Jolting along the badly paved
main streets of Terrasini we catch sight of courts and
alleys opening off it which once again make us think of
Tunis. The white houses are low and square with flat
roofs ; some have only a door and no windows facing
the street, where dark-eyed, curly-headed children are

Trapani

playing in the dust. Few women are in evidence and those few are shrouded in black or Paisley-pattern shawls, while the men wear rugs on their shoulders or voluminous cloaks with the hoods drawn up burnous fashion.

After the larger towns of Partenico and Alcamo (the latter prides itself on having given birth to Ciullo d' Alcamo the poet), the road crosses the railway line where a tiny station bears the name Segesta ; some time after this a majestic temple comes in sight, standing high in solitary grandeur on its flowery platform among the mountains. How marvellously perfect it appears against the grey-green background ! Surely that wondrous sanctuary was raised by demigods, not by mere men !

The road now winds along the base of the mountains among fields of corn and crimson clover ; then crossing a fertile plain, passes under the shadow of Monte San Giuliano and enters the suburbs of Trapani.

Trapani, situated at the north-west extremity of Sicily, might well be called the " City of the Four Winds," for there the wind, damp and cold or hot and steamy according to the season, never ceases blowing. A glance at the map will show the exposed position of the town, which stands on a narrow, sickle-shaped peninsula— hence its ancient name of Drepana, from *drepanon*, a sickle. The saline or salt lagoons which form the chief industry of Trapani stretch for miles along the flat shore, where numerous windmills connected with the salt works give a momentary illusion of being in Holland, until Mount Eryx looming near, its summit wreathed in clouds, recalls the fact that we are in Sicily, the land of classic myth and legend.

Drepana, like Zancle (Messina), is said to have been

History

founded by Kronos or Saturn, who let fall his sickle there. Its first inhabitants, far back in the dawn of time, were probably Sicanians or Cyclopians. Later, as the port of Eryx on the neighbouring mountain, it was well known to the Phœnicians, who called it Darban, a sting, or goad. Here Æneas landed to bury his father Anchises and again on his return from Carthage to hold funeral games in his honour, in which the island now called Asinello was the goal for the boat races, as described in the Æneid (Books III and V).

It is only in 260 B.C. that Trapani takes a definite place in history as distinct from legend. In that year the city sided with the Carthaginians and welcomed Hamilcar Barca within its walls. It was besieged by the Romans in 249 and finally fell under their dominion, together with Eryx, Lilybæum and Panormus, in 242, when the burning of the Carthaginian fleet off the Ægadian Islands ended the First Punic War. Peace was signed on the island of Marittimo, and Drepanum became a consular city, but it gradually waned in importance as Lilybæum, now Marsala, absorbed the commerce of Sicily.

During the Roman domination a large colony of Jews settled in the district still called Giudecca. A picturesque tower and façade in this part of the city show the mingling of Saracen and Norman architecture peculiar to Sicily.

The Saracens, who ruled for many years in Trapani, were finally defeated by Jourdain, the son of Count Roger, who took the city by a bold stroke.

During the Crusades Trapani returned to importance and became a depot for all ships sailing to the Holy Land.

Charles of Anjou was unpopular in this part of the island, and a number of Trapanese met together with

Photo

Ballance

THE TEMPLE, SEGESTA

This glorious temple of golden sandstone stands in majestic solitude on a flowery platform among the mountains.

History

Giovanni di Procida at the Scoglio di Mal Consiglio to conspire against the French and offer the crown to Peter of Aragon. After the massacre of the Sicilian Vespers the Trapanese rose against their French governor and put him to death.

Peter of Aragon landed here on September 18th, 1282, and was proclaimed King of Sicily. Several of the Aragonese sovereigns sojourned in Trapani, which, like Messina, was granted the privilege of a Consulate in Tunis. It was at this time that the salt beds were established and became a source of wealth to the city.

The Emperor Charles V landed at Trapani after his victory at Tunis in 1535, and in the church of Sant' Agostino swore a solemn oath to maintain the privileges granted to the city and to Sicily.

From this time onward Trapani was wholly given up to her flourishing trade in salt, her tunny fisheries and other industries, among which were the cutting of coral and precious stones, pottery and wood-carving.

Trapani was the first Sicilian city to rise against the Bourbons in 1848 and took an active part in the Revolution of 1860. A Trapanese fisherman, Strazzera, warned Garibaldi of the presence of the Bourbon ships and advised him to land at Marsala. The Erycene and Trapanese troops were the first to join the Thousand at Calatafimi and distinguished themselves at Volturno.

Trapani has been the birthplace of many famous men, among them the composer, Alessandro Scarlatti (1659–1725).

As we wander through the narrow, well-kept streets we are reminded that this city is said to be the cleanest in Sicily; but its neighbour, San Giuliano, the little town on the mountain-top, seems to us even more worthy of this distinction!

Churches

Trapani possesses many handsome buildings in a variety of styles, baroque predominating, though both here and at San Giuliano we come upon graceful windows of Saracen-Norman design and traces of XVIth-century influence are also visible. Several of the churches are interesting either for their architecture or for the artistic treasures they contain.

Sant' Agostino was built by the Templars in the XIVth century, but little of the original building remains except a fine door and a delicate rose window.

San Nicolò (formerly dell' Assunzione) was founded by Belisarius and belonged originally to the Greek rite.

Trapani was one of the first Sicilian cities to embrace Christianity ; the church of San Pietro stands on the spot where St. Peter is believed to have preached, causing the people to turn from the worship of Poseidon, to whom it was their custom to sacrifice the largest tunny caught during the year. It was in this church that Peter of Aragon took his oath. He is said to have lived in a modest house near the church, to show that he did not come as a conqueror but as the friend of the people.

The Oratorio di San Michele contains eighteen groups of painted wooden figures, remarkable for their realism and beauty of expression, representing the scenes of the Passion. They are of XVIIth-century workmanship and are carried in the Procession of the Mysteries, which leaves the church at 3 p.m. on Good Friday, accompanied by a band and by most of the population, and only re-enters at 7 a.m. on the following morning !

Some way outside Trapani on the road to Monte San Giuliano is the famous sanctuary of Maria Santissima, the Madonna dell' Annunziata, a shrine to which the faithful flock in large numbers. This Madonna is specially invoked for protection against the perils of the

Madonna of Trapani

deep, though the collection of quaint votive pictures in the sacristy proclaim her power to avert many other forms of danger.

On entering the church, which was built in 1322 with later additions and restored in 1760, one is struck by its bareness, unusual in the sacred edifices of Sicily. The decoration is entirely concentrated in a magnificently carved marble arch, the work of Gagini, and in the bronze gates behind which the miraculous image is preserved.

We approach the altar and gaze at the exquisite figure standing above it, under a *baldacchino* supported by eight marble columns with Corinthian capitals—a graceful female form with the Child on her arm ; and we are overwhelmed with surprise, not only at her beauty, but at her unlikeness to any of the usual Madonna types. Carved by a master hand in creamy Oriental marble, her almond eyes look down upon us and her lips curve in an enigmatical smile more reminiscent of Venus than of Mary ! A sense of Pagan mystery rather than of Christian mysticism seems to brood over her, and a doubt as to her identity flickers through our minds. The statue is said to have come from Cyprus, so . . . who knows ?

There is a tradition that Guerregio, the Knight of Jerusalem who brought the statue to Trapani in 1291, had caused it to be made by the Pisani in his native city, Pisa, and had taken it with him to the East, but fearing lest it should fall into the hands of the Saracens he brought it back, and, his ship being caught in a storm off the Sicilian coast, vowed to leave the precious image where he first touched land. However this may be, the statue has little in common with the work of the Pisani.

This exquisite work of art gains in beauty from the severity of its surroundings ; one would like to relieve the two graceful heads of the heavy jewelled crowns which seem to weigh them down, and which would be better in the Museum with the other jewels of the Madonna—a costly patrimony of votive offerings.

The Museum is in a disused monastery adjoining the church ; a fine building with richly inlaid marble staircase and charming cloisters. Besides the jewels and an extensive collection of ecclesiastical vestments, it contains a picture gallery and many interesting objects, arranged with excellent taste and care. In a room on the ground floor stands the authentic guillotine which did its grim work in Trapani at a comparatively recent date. The mechanism, though somewhat primitive, was none the less effective, and the sight of this grisly relic produces a thrill of horror.

A motor drive of less than two hours brings us to the summit of Monte San Giuliano, where, at a height of 2500 feet, the curious little town occupies the site of the ancient Eryx, whose origin is lost in the mists of antiquity. The Greeks believed it to have been founded by Heracles. The Phœnicians fortified it, and some of their walls, composed of massive blocks, are still standing. On the site of the temple of Phœnician Astarte, Æneas raised one to Aphrodite, or Venus Erycina, who was worshipped by all the peoples of the Mediterranean. Nothing is now left of this temple but a few foundations and a ruined reservoir called the Fountain of Venus, within a flower-carpeted enclosure. Close by is the Ponte di Dedalo, an arch said to have been built by Dædalus when he flew with his son Icarus from Crete to Sicily. It can only be seen by leaning over a dizzy chasm.

Although these remains are so slight, the lover of classical lore finds it quite worth his while to ascend the

Photo   *Brog*

MONTE SAN GIULIANO NEAR TRAPANI

A mediaeval castle crowns the summit of the ancient Mount Eryx. Spanning the chasm is the arch
said to have been built by Daedalus ; Villa Pepoli perches on a crag.

The Cleanest Town in Sicily

mountain and spend an hour or two dreaming in this silent spot, whose moss-grown stones could tell strange tales of those remote days when, for Greek and Phœnician alike, this enclosure on the mountain-top was a holy place.

On entering the town by the Trapani Gate, we pass the cathedral, an old building much restored, and, climbing towards the mediæval castle whose towers rise near the ruins, lose our way in a labyrinth of narrow streets, spotlessly clean, many of them paved in neat patterns of black and white, and wholly deserted. Where are the inhabitants ? we ask our guide, if we have had the forethought to engage one on arrival. He explains that the men—those who are left, for the war dealt heavily with this small town, as the long list of names on the Monument proves—are away in the fields, for the population is largely agricultural. As for the women, they stay indoors and have not even the curiosity to look out at the sound of footsteps. This is disappointing, for they are noted for their beauty ! On the rare occasions when they appear in the street, they wear a picturesque mantle of black silk, rather like a domino, which covers the head and drapes the figure, its voluminous folds being held in place by one hand. The effect of this graceful costume is decidedly Spanish.

From the castle tower a magnificent view may be enjoyed. At out feet lies Trapani, its sickle-like shape distinctly visible from this height, together with the flat expanse of salt beds intersected by channels. A smiling plain dotted with villages stretches away to the east, where Monte Cofano rises abruptly from the sea, forming a pendant to Monte San Giuliano and the other horn of a wide bay, while the long range of San Vito bounds the horizon. To the west the Ægadian Islands,

The Madonna of Custonaci

Marittimo, Levanzo and Favignana, float on the blue African Sea ; to the south lies Marsala. On exceptionally clear days the island of Pantelleria, half-way to Africa, is visible, and sometimes even Cape Bon, near Tunis. A truly glorious panorama.

Monte San Giuliano (whose modern name tradition attributes to a vision of the Saint putting the Saracens to flight, seen by Count Roger when besieging the town), is a favourite summer resort with the Trapanese ; in winter its climate is damp and foggy ; one wonders how the inhabitants endure it in their comfortless homes, few of which are provided with any means of heating.

In a corner of the Public Gardens which crown the precipitous side of the mountain, we come upon a praying stone facing Custonaci, a village on a rock which rises out of the plain. Here is the shrine of the famous Madonna of Custonaci, who is appealed to in times of drought or other disaster and is as powerful on land as the Madonna of Trapani is at sea. At intervals the sacred picture, said to have been painted by St. Luke, is brought in solemn procession, hung round with jewels, to Monte San Giuliano, and installed in the cathedral, where it has sometimes remained for a period of years, its departure being an occasion of lamentation and mourning for the inhabitants. When the Madonna is at Custonaci the praying stone in the gardens is constantly occupied.

Henry Festing Jones and other writers on Sicilian customs have found a parallel between these peregrinations of the Madonna to and from the mountain and the flittings of Venus Erycina and her predecessor Astarte between Sicily and Carthage. And indeed we find many of these parallels in the history of religion, as race succeeds race and new forms of worship take the place of the old.

CHAPTER V

THE traditional games, dances and amusements of
a people provide a fruitful field for study, since they
have a large share in the formation of the national
character, which they in turn reflect and portray. This
is the case to an unusual degree with the Marionette
Theatre or *Opra ri Pupi*, which is perhaps the most
characteristic, the most interesting historically and
ethnologically, of all Sicilian institutions.

This primitive form of drama is believed to have been
introduced from France about the XIIIth century. It
took deep root in Sicily and has reached there the highest
point of its evolution, becoming a really important art
and a not unworthy successor to the Greek Drama which
once flourished on Sicilian soil. It may appear a
daring statement, but a close and sympathetic study of
these two forms of art, apparently at opposite poles,
reveals more than one point of contact between them ;
and from the *Teatrino* of Piazza San Cosimo in Palermo
to the vast Greek Theatre of Syracuse is not such a far
cry as would at first sight appear !

That fatalistic sense conveyed by the tragedies of
Æschylus and Sophocles, of men and women, like
puppets in the hands of inexorable Fate, moving surely,
involuntarily and inevitably towards a predestined end,
is present in miniature in the dramas of heroism and
magic performed by the little wooden figures whose

actions are controlled by their Destiny in the wings. The tragic and comic masks of the ancients, expressive in their grotesque painted immobility, find their counterpart in the stolid wooden faces of the Paladins. Another point of resemblance lies in the high and noble sentiments expressed, often bombastically, by the actors—sentiments which are not without their influence on the mind and character of the frequenters of the *Teatrino*, as they doubtless had their share in moulding the character of the warriors and philosophers of ancient Greece.

The Marionette Theatre during all the centuries of its existence has drawn its inspiration from the age-long conflict between Christian and Saracen, in which Sicily was one of the chief battlefields, and from all that heroic-romantic literature which sprang from the *Chanson de Roland*.

Roland or Orlando, the invincible warrior, the perfect knight, slayer of dragons, champion of beauty in distress, is the hero of nearly all Marionette dramas ; his prowess is legendary as that of Achilles, his ultimate doom as certain.

And it is on these deeds of valour, these high sentiments of chivalry and virtuous protection of the weaker sex, that Sicilian boys are nourished from infancy, just as the youth of more civilised (?) countries is brought up on detective stories and films of adventure and crime. What wonder then that the average Sicilian, with all his hot southern blood, his jealousy and violence of revenge, has in him a strain of old-fashioned chivalry and romance which makes him a brave soldier, a devoted lover and a faithful friend ?

Every town in Sicily has its Marionette Theatre, the larger ones two or three. Often these are barn-like buildings, though occasionally they have some preten-

A COURTYARD SCENE IN TRAPANI

Many families live in rooms overlooking this courtyard of an old palace.
They enjoy gossiping from window to window and on the stairs.

sions to a theatrical appearance. There are usually several performances every evening, each lasting from one to two hours, a new episode in the serial drama being given every evening. Often a series will last for two or three months, the audience returning night after night and following the story with breathless interest. They have even been known to protest so vigorously against the death of a favourite hero, that the story has had to be altered and prolonged in order to give him a new lease of life !

In the case of Orlando, when the scene of his death is reached, the theatre is apt to be half empty, a great portion of the audience feeling unable to endure the emotional strain of the final tragedy. Some of the younger devotees of the *Teatrino* are not even aware that their hero must go the way of all flesh, and to our question as to when the death of Orlando would take place a small enthusiast aged about six replied in a shocked tone :

" Orlando ? Ma Orlando non muore *mai !* " (Orlando ? But Orlando *never* dies !)

The theatre is generally crowded with men and boys, for as we remarked before, Sicilian women of the middle and lower classes are seldom seen in public places.

During the long wait before the drama begins (punctuality is not a virtue of the Marionette Theatre !) and in the intervals between the acts, the piercing cry of " *A-gua ! A-gua !* " " *Si-men-za ! Si-men-za !* " is heard above the hubbub of conversation, and two boys push their way between the benches, the one handing round a large tumbler of water which he replenishes from an Arabian-looking brass vessel like an elongated coffee-pot, the other offering packets of dried melon seed. The cool drink is welcomed to quench the thirst produced by the

The Marionettes

seeds (*simenza*), which they chew incessantly, cracking them deftly with their teeth. When the boys become too uproarious a man in the front benches restores order by hitting them with a short truncheon. A wheezy hurdy-gurdy takes the place of an orchestra and grinds out cheerful tunes at every pause in the performance, the player taking his cue from a whistle or the stamping of a foot in the wings.

The decoration of the theatre is primitive in the extreme. Outside the door are flaring posters showing in crude but effective design the most sensational episodes in the drama. The drop scene usually represents a battle. The scenery is often very good, the pillared hall of Charlemagne's palace being generally in excellent perspective and forming a telling background for the martial figures who strut across the stage.

But all these primitive surroundings do not in the least prepare the stranger for the genuine art and thrilling realism of the performance. From the rise of the curtain to its final fall he is held spellbound by the drama enacted by these puppets less than three feet high, whose stolid countenances and jerky movements make a curious emotional appeal, often, it is true, provoking laughter, but sometimes even moving to tears.

At first sight the marionettes appear to be nearly life-size, the illusion being caused by the low opening of the proscenium, and it is hardly destroyed by the occasional unwary appearance of a gigantic human hand or foot protruding from the wings ; to be really convinced of their smallness and great proportional weight (13–14 lbs.), the spectator must hold one in his hand and try to work its wires.

Here is a typical performance at the *Teatrino* in Piazza San Cosimo, Palermo.

A WANDERING MUSICIAN

This Sicilian accordion player would not dream of starting out without a large green umbrella slung gunwise over his shoulder. Many a tarantella is danced to the inspiriting strains of his " organino."

The Marionettes

The knight Ruggero, after saving from the fury of the Saracens a Princess whom he finds wandering in a forest, craves hospitality of Pinamonte, a ferocious-looking individual, who ogles the Princess and offers them a banquet, after which they retire to rest. Ruggero is seen in white under-garments devoutly saying his prayers and climbing into bed, where he falls asleep, breathing heavily.

Enter Pinamonte who announces : " Now I will slay him and take the maiden for myself ! " and strikes the sleeping knight repeatedly with his sword. Ruggero awakes crying "Traitor ! " rolls on to the floor and lies there dead, his shirt falling open by an ingenious contrivance and revealing his chest all streaked with blood.

In the next scene Charlemagne is expressing to the assembled knights his anxiety at Ruggero's prolonged absence, when the Princess, having somehow escaped from the clutches of Pinamonte, bursts upon the scene with news of the murder. Charlemagne weeps copiously and loudly for the death of his knight and sends Orlando with a picked band to avenge him. The departure of the Paladins forms an impressive scene. With a martial clanking they stamp round the stage and go out one by one, the last to go being Gano di Magonza, the traitor, represented by a marionette much smaller than the rest, not, as might be imagined, because he is a dwarf, but as a naïve form of caricature, since this well-known personage, who figures in most of the Carlovingian dramas, is hated by the frequenters of the *Opira di Pupi*

Next comes the assembling of Pinamonte's forces, and a realistic series of duels takes place, making up the battle and reminding one of the duels between the captains in the Iliad. Heads roll about the stage, bodies are split lengthwise and fall writhing on the heap of

The Greco Family

slain. Orlando the invincible performs prodigies of valour ; and finally Pinamonte's castle is seen in flames while large stones crash down upon the stage and the audience goes wild with delight.

A comic scene of clowns, acrobats or ballet generally closes the performance, which must be seen to be appreciated, so extraordinary is the effect of all these complicated actions performed by puppets at the bidding of two men in the wings, who also speak the parts with clever changes of voice.   There are, of course, some amusing anachronisms which only add to the quaint charm of the entertainment, such, for instance, as the occasional appearance of Orlando wearing a tricolour sash across his shining cuirass, like a provincial *sindaco* at a wedding ! Vultures, serpents and mythical monsters lurk in dark forests to test the valour of solitary knights.

The *Opira di Pupi* is a traditional art handed down from father to son, at any rate in its two principal homes, Palermo and Catania.   In Palermo it is in the hands of the talented Greco family.   Don Gaetano Greco, born in 1813, invented the " armoured marionettes," the really magnificent figures now in use, and introduced many mechanical improvements, among them " lateral manipulation " (from the wings).   Before his time the puppets were less lifelike and were worked from above, from a " bridge," as they still are in Catania and several other places.

Don Gaetano's theatre was in the Piazza Nuova (the Market), but it has passed into other hands and is only open intermittently.   The original decoration was retained and there was an attempt at raised boxes of primitive form, their panels well painted somewhat in the style of the old marriage chests, with scenes from the Story of the Paladins.   The seats in most of these

THE TEMPLE OF CONCORD, GIRGENTI

At sunset these Doric columns are ablaze with gold, and between them we get glimpses of green hills and fields, gleaming like emerald in the evening light.

The Greco Family

theatres are high narrow benches on which it is difficult to maintain one's equilibrium.

Don Gaetano was a Garibaldian hero, and his wife too was noted for her patriotism. His marionettes were considered so marvellous that a legend grew up round them. It was said that they were really endowed with life, and that their creator's one obsession was to produce a puppet gifted with speech. At last he made one, Bradamante, so human in expression and movements that he exclaimed, gazing at it in delight :

" Oh, if you could only speak ! "

At this appeal the puppet moved its head, rolled its eyes and articulated the word " *Ma ! . . .*" Don Gaetano, in the shock of seeing his dream realised, lost his reason.

His descendants declare, however, that all this is mere legend and that Don Gaetano died in full possession of his faculties at the age of sixty-one (1874).

His son, Don Achille, followed in his footsteps, studying, inventing, perfecting and loving his marionettes as though they were his children. The war hit him hard ; his two sons were under arms and he could not continue alone ; the theatre was closed, the marionettes dispersed. But brighter days dawned and the theatre in the Piazza San Cosimo was opened with only thirteen marionettes. By degrees the " troupe " was increased to several hundred, and the management was taken over by Don Achille's talented sons, Alessandro and Ermenegildo.

Don Achille still continued to take part in the performances and to devote himself to the preparation of certain pyrotechnic specialities—his own jealously guarded secret—for the scenes of magic and enchantment. Those who have had the good fortune to see him preserve a vivid memory of the tall, distinguished-looking old

The Greco Family

man standing at the door of the theatre and welcoming his public with the courteous manner of a prince receiving guests in his palace.

The Greco marionettes are so skilfully manipulated that they really walk step by step and in their duels use genuine sword-play. I have often seen Ermenegildo, at the close of a performance where foreigners were present, bring Orlando down into the auditorium, and placing the little figure on a bench, cause him to make his bow, with hand on heart, and then kneeling on one knee, kiss the hand of a lady visitor. It is a strange sensation to have one's hand reverently kissed by the great Orlando, the *preux chevalier* whose valour one has just witnessed! A regular frequenter and student of this *teatrino* ends by feeling a personal affection for these wooden heroes, scarcely inferior to that felt for them by their owners and creators.

Tradition decrees that Orlando must be represented with a squint. Two explanations are given for this fact; one being that it denotes ferocity, the other that the hero acquired it as a boy from gazing in awe and wonder at his uncle Charlemagne.

In Catania the marionette tradition is as strong as in Palermo. The well-known actors Angelo Musco and Giovanni Grasso began life as *pupari*, and Grasso's father and grandfather had a celebrated *teatrino*. The mantle then fell upon Don Sebastiano Zappalà, a simple, unaffected son of the people, who achieved fame by his creation of really marvellous marionettes measuring over four feet and weighing from 56 to 90 lbs., made entirely by himself, even to the elaborately embossed devices on their armour. Owing to their weight they have to be manipulated from a " bridge." Instead of the parts being spoken by the manipulators, they are

Photo

A ROAD NEAR TAORMINA

The sun-baked road and ox-cart, the tall *agave* bending from the tangle of vegetation above the wall, and Etna in the distance form a typically Sicilian landscape.

Sport & General

The Libretto

read, Don Raffaele Trombetta, an old *puparo* with a
fine voice and fifty years' experience in the profession,
being a celebrated reader, whose name ranks with that
of Zappalà in the annals of the *teatrino*.

Trombetta formerly had his own theatre and the
marionette hero Uzeda was his creation. This legendary
personage occupies in the hearts of the Catania populace
an equal place with Orlando. The original of Uzeda was
Don Giovanni Francesco Paceco, Duke of Uzeda and
Viceroy of Sicily in 1687.

An interesting feature of this art is the libretto, which
though drawn principally from *I Paladini di Francia,
Orlando Furioso, Guerin Meschino*, etc., is generally
written either by the proprietor of the *teatrino* or by
someone connected with it, often quite a humble man who
though he may have had little schooling, is well versed
in the history of chivalry and saturated with all the
literature of the Carlovingian cycle. Thus his fertile
and poetic imagination can add new episodes and invent
new generations of warriors to eke out the old stories,
while his dialogue, though not always free from gram-
matical errors, is invariably in the grandiose, pompous
style of Tasso and Ariosto. The Paladin dramas are
always in Italian, the comic scenes often in dialect.

Much has been written on the subject of the *Opra ri
Pupi*. Giovanni Verga has immortalised it in his *Don
Candeloro*, Salvator Lo Presti gives the history of the
Catania theatres in his illustrated pamphlet *I Pupi*,
and Yorick in *La Storia dei Burattini* traces the history
of the Marionette Theatre all over Europe. For English
readers there are Henry Festing Jones' three inimitable
volumes, *Diversions in Sicily, Castellinaria and other
Sicilian Diversions, Mount Eryx and other Diversions of
Travels*.

The Public Story-Teller

But no description, however eloquent, can really convey an adequate idea of the fascination, charm and originality of this form of art.

We must not close this chapter without referring to another mediæval survival in the amusements of Palermo. This is the *Contastorie di Piazza*, or public story-teller. These story-tellers are a familiar sight in Tunis and other Oriental cities, and their presence in Palermo is no doubt a survival of the Saracen dominion in Sicily.

The *Contastorie* holds his court in a kind of barn in the Piazza Castello, near the harbour. He stands on a small platform and his audience, composed chiefly of old men, sits gazing at him with wrapt expression while he declaims with melodramatic fervour a chapter of some serial story in which high-sounding titles largely figure. During this first part of the programme the stranger in search of local colour feels a slight sense of disappointment, especially as the story-teller is a commonplace-looking man, not even very old, and clad in everyday garments. But when he embarks on the second part, the story of the Paladins, all is changed. His voice deepens, his eyes flash, his hair seems to stand on end, Brandishing a flat wooden sword, the age-long emblem of the heroic story-teller, he gesticulates so violently as almost to fall off his narrow platform. In ringing tones he recites the glories of Roland and Charlemagne, of Rinaldo and Fortebraccio. The audience wakes up and applauds. . . . The habitué of the Marionette Theatre sees once more the knights in their shining armour and floating plumes. . . . The commonplace story-teller is transfigured, and we are back in the time of the Crusades, living through the glorious adventures of the heroes who have become our personal friends.

CHAPTER VI

IT is strange how a few hours' journey by train or motor-car from Norman-Saracen Palermo will transport us into another world—the world of ancient Greece, where the tales of mythology seem as natural and acceptable as everyday facts; where the spirit of the Golden Age still haunts the glorious ruins and where for the seeing eye temples and theatres are once more peopled with the white-robed figures of the past.

Scarcely in Greece itself is this feeling more vivid than in Sicily, where these marvellous remains of other days seem to blend and become one with the natural beauty of their setting. Very specially is this the case with the Temple of Segesta, which may be reached from Palermo in three hours. The road takes us through sun-baked villages, over wild mountain passes and, after Partenico, through smiling, fertile country; crossing the bridge built in 1926 over the river Gaggera (Scamander), it ends at a short distance from the temple. The makers of this road realised the sacredness of the precincts to which it leads, and so planned it that no noise of modern traffic should intrude on the solemn silence of the great temple.

A footpath leads up the easy slope and brings us to a green plateau starred with many-coloured flowers and tufted with great bushes of wild fennel. There stands the temple of golden sandstone, faultless in form, sublime in its mountain solitude. Through a gap in the hills to

71

The Temple

the north we get a glimpse of turquoise sea, while away inland the mountains are piled up peak above peak round the wild heart of Sicily.

On the far side the plateau ends abruptly above a rocky gorge cleft by some primeval convulsion. Looking over the edge we expect to see a foaming torrent below, but the watercourse is now dry.

It would be difficult to find a more ideal spot whereon to build a sanctuary. Before this masterpiece of Doric architecture words fail and thought itself seems suspended. We can only gaze, throwing open all the receptive channels of our being to the manifold influences of the place— those strange forces of Nature which were so real and tangible to the ancients that they endowed them with personality and worshipped them as divinities. Some such perception must have led the founders of Segesta to build their city on Monte Barbaro and their temple on this upland platform. We would gladly know which of the deities of Olympus was worshipped in this perfect shrine; but hitherto the great temple has refused to reveal its secret with any certainty. It is thought that it may have been dedicated either to Demeter or Artemis, and the story of a bronze statue of the former goddess carried off by the Carthaginians, restored by Scipio Africanus and again removed by Verres, lends colour to the supposition that the Earth Mother was worshipped in this splendid fane.

According to legend the city of Segesta was founded by Elymos, the son of Anchises and brother of Eryx, or by his descendants, the Elymians, a Trojan race, in the XIIth century B.C. In time it became completely Hellenised and the temple was built by Dorian architects in the Vth century B.C. Its proportions are perfect, but it was never finished, for the thirty-six columns are unfluted, the metopes unadorned by sculpture, and it lacks the usual cella.

Segesta was never on good terms with the other Greek cities of Sicily, perhaps on account of her Trojan origin, or more probably because from the earliest times she had been closely in touch with the Phœnicians. Twice she nearly caused the ruin of the Greek cause in the island ; first in 415 B.C. when by appealing to Athens for help against her rival and deadly enemy, Selinus, she brought about the ill-fated Athenian expedition against Syracuse ; and again in 409 B.C. when she summoned the Carthaginians to her aid, with the result that Selinus was destroyed by Hannibal.

It is related that when the Segestans appealed to the Athenians for aid, these took the precaution of sending representatives to discover if the city were in a position to pay for the help demanded. The Segestans were really very poor, but by dint of borrowing gold and silver vessels from the neighbouring towns they succeeded in making such a fine show with their sacred treasures and rich banquets that the ambassadors departed satisfied as to the flourishing condition of the city. After their defeat the Athenians were not in a position to enforce the promised payment, otherwise Segesta might have paid dearly for the fraud practised on her allies !

In 307 Segesta was taken by Agathocles, Tyrant of Syracuse, who caused 10,000 of the inhabitants to be treacherously massacred on the banks of the Scamander and all the youth of the city to be sold as slaves. He tortured the rich men until they revealed the hiding-place of their treasures, after which they were put to death and the city razed to the ground. It was probably at this time of disaster that work on the temple was suspended never to be resumed.

Selinus

But Agathocles paid with his life for this treachery towards Segesta. His favourite slave, a Segestan who had beheld the destruction of the city, waited for sixteen years to accomplish his vengeance, and at last succeeded in administering a subtle poison which caused his master to die a lingering and agonising death. When Agathocles was past speech this slave and others who hated the tyrant laid him still breathing upon the funeral pyre. And thus the hapless victims of Segesta were avenged.

In the First Punic War the city allied herself with Rome, to whom her Trojan origin appealed, as the Romans themselves claimed descent from Æneas.

A steep mule path leads to the summit of Monte Barbaro, where the Greek Theatre is hewn out of the face of the rock in a magnificent position. The stage and semicircle of seats are well preserved and the view of sea and mountains is superb. The temple seen from this height has the appearance of a delicately perfect model building. The town of Segesta was evidently on the mountain-top, like so many others of early foundation ; remains of houses with Greek and Roman pavements have been found. Down below in the Scamander Valley are traces of baths supplied by four hot springs.

About two hours by road or railway from Segesta brings us to Castelvetrano. The road passes near the historic battlefield of Calatafimi, where, on the 15th of May, 1860, Garibaldi's Thousand, with romantic courage worthy of the heroes of the Iliad, charged uphill in the face of the Bourbon guns and put the enemy to flight.

It is advisable to sleep at Castelvetrano, in order to devote a whole day to the marvellous ruins of Selinunte, which are within easy reach of the town.

Selinus, now Selinunte, was so named from the wild parsley (*selinon*) which grew luxuriantly in the valley

74

Sack & Destruction

below the town. A greater contrast to Segesta cannot be imagined, for here instead of one perfect temple we have an entire city in ruins, desolate and sad, but intensely interesting. By a careful study of the fallen stones, helped by a little imagination, we may piece the whole together and form a clear idea of the topography and life of an ancient Greek city.

Selinus was the westernmost Greek colony in Sicily and the nearest to Africa; it was founded in 628 B.C. by colonists from Megara Hyblea on high ground facing the African sea, and soon became a flourishing city, pushing its commercial relations as far as Acre, which had a Selinus Gate. It suffered, however, from malaria and its political position was always precarious, situated as it was between the powerful states of Akragas, Segesta and Motye, the latter belonging to the Phœnicians and Carthaginians. It was continually at war with Segesta and suffered from the fierce contest between Greeks and Carthaginians, siding with one or the other as political necessity dictated. Finally in 409 B.C. the Carthaginians, summoned by the Segestans, laid siege to Selinus and took it after a heroic defence lasting nine days. The African general Hannibal Gisgon (grandson of Hamilcar, who perished at the battle of Himera), had spent his youth in exile at Selinus and was full of vindictive bitterness against the city. So when it fell into his power he ferociously ordered its complete destruction. Of the inhabitants, 16,000, including women, were put to the sword and 5000 taken to Africa as slaves; the remaining 2500 fled to Akragas. The city was sacked and burnt in spite of the remonstrances of the Syracusans, who sent messengers to Hannibal entreating him to set free the prisoners and spare the temples. The Carthaginian general replied roughly that citizens who had been incapable of defending their liberty could learn to live in slavery, and that it was useless to protect the temples since the Gods had deserted them.

Traces of fire are still visible on the fallen columns, but surely no human agency alone, not even the fury of Hannibal's barbarian army, could have brought about such a complete overthrow, in which hardly one stone remained upon another. An earthquake of which no definite account has come down to us evidently completed the ruin of the lordly temples, whose massive columns lie prone all in the same direction. This cannot be the work of man; the almost symmetrical arrangement of the ruins points to some far greater force which shook a city to pieces like a house of cards.

Thus the magnificent city with its seven or eight temples ceased to exist within two centuries from its foundation. An attempt to restore it was made in 407 B.C by Hermocrates, the exiled Syracusan patriot, but his small colony was finally destroyed in the First Punic War (250 B.C.). Later a few Christian hermits built their huts among the ruins and the Saracens made a stand there against King Roger, calling the desolate spot Rahal-el-Asnam or Village of the Idols. Desolate it has remained through the centuries, a gigantic heap of ruins; but archæologists consider it one of the most interesting examples of a Greek city.

In 1823 the Englishmen Harriss and Angell began to excavate and their work has been continued by others; the metopes and inscriptions found are now in the Museum at Palermo. A few years ago nine columns of the Temple of Heracles were raised with the cornice to their original position and stand sharply outlined against the blue southern sky, a landmark amid the surrounding desolation.

THE ENTRANCE TO CATACOMBS, SYRACUSE

The entrance to the Catacombs is in this church of San Giovanni. Close by is an ancient basilica in
whose crypt St. Paul is said to have preached.

The Acropolis & Temples

The largest group of ruins belongs to the Acropolis, but the city extended some way to the north and possessed no less than three necropoli ; these, together with the suburbs, were covered by the shifting sand-dunes which are a phenomenon of this coast and proclaim the nearness of the African desert.

The Acropolis contains the four most ancient temples, called A, B, C, D, in the absence of any certainty as to the divinities to whom they were dedicated. The circuit of the walls is still traceable and the line of two main streets with others branching off from them at right angles. Of the four temples the oldest and largest is C, which stood on the highest point of the Acropolis and was approached by a flight of nine steps. It was probably built at the foundation of the city, and the three oldest metopes belonged to it. This temple is remarkably long in proportion to its width and some of the huge columns are monoliths. It is thought to have been dedicated to Heracles.

Adjoining Temple C is the small Temple B, which beside its gigantic neighbour seems like a miniature model of a temple ; it has Ionic columns with Doric entablature, while all the other temples are pure Doric ; it was covered with coloured stucco and may have been built in honour of Empedocles, the philosopher who drained the marshy valley to make the city healthy, and to whom the grateful citizens wished to render divine honours.

Besides the temples of the Acropolis there are remains of square towers and other buildings, showing that the main city stood on this spot. On a hill at some distance to the east are three more temples but no other remains. Of these temples, E, F, G, inscriptions found in their precincts show that E was dedicated to Hera and G to

Temple of Demeter

Apollo, the protector of Selinus. This colossal temple, the third largest known, was never finished; most of the columns are unfluted, and some gigantic blocks from the quarries of Rocca di Cusa, each weighing 100 tons, are lying near the temple. Several great drums (sections of columns), similar to those among the ruins, are still lying at the bottom of the quarry, while others may be seen along the road to Selinunte. The stone for building the city was taken from these quarries; evidently work there was suddenly stopped at the time of the Carthaginian invasion and never resumed.

All the temples of Selinus faced the rising sun and E must have been one of the most perfect examples of Doric architecture.

Across the valley of the Selino or Madione to the west of the Acropolis we find some other interesting remains. Within the walls of a sacred enclosure is a temple of Demeter; before it stands a large sacrificial altar. More than 5000 terra-cotta statuettes were found here and it is thought to have been a mortuary station where funeral processions halted; it is on the way to an immense necropolis.

This Demeter worship near Selinus is significant; the country, notwithstanding its unhealthiness, was extremely fertile and produced a fine quality of corn which was largely exported. The city possessed a fleet and its coinage is exceptionally rich; much of it bears the emblem of the wild parsley.

The metopes from the temples of Selinunte show that while Greek architecture had reached its highest development in the Vth century B.C. sculpture was still in its infancy—archaic in design and execution, but having a vivacious sense of movement. One of the metopes from Temple C represents Perseus slaying Medusa

A SUNLIT DOORWAY IN A SICILIAN VILLAGE

Sicilians are sun worshippers, and love to bask in their deity's golden rays.
This peasant's gouty-looking shoes are a very usual kind of footwear.

while Athena looks on approvingly. The Gorgon is a grotesque figure whose hideous face wears a satisfied grin as her head is being sawn off ! The others represent a Quadriga, and Heracles carrying the dwarfs Cercopes suspended head downwards from a pole ; these are all of the VIth century.

The metopes from Temple E show great progress in design and execution ; they are of the Vth century, the epoch of Phidias. They represent Heracles slaying Hippolyta ; Zeus and Hera ; and Athena slaying a giant.

The two metopes from Temple F, representing Europa on the bull and a Sphinx, are of a later period and may possibly have been brought from Greece.

From Selinunte we proceed to Girgenti, passing through Sciacca (Arabic Shakkah), once the haunt of brigands, but now a quiet and prosperous town. Sciacca possesses a well-preserved circuit of walls and the remains of two old castles of the Luna and Perollo families, whose feuds disturbed the town from 1410 to 1524 and were known as *I casi di Sciacca*. The cathedral was founded by a daughter of King Roger and contains a statue by the sculptor Laurana.

At a short distance from Sciacca are the vapour baths of San Calogero, believed in early days to have been founded by Dædalus ; in the Middle Ages the discovery of their virtues was attributed to San Calogero.

The XVIth-century historian Tommaso Fazello was a native of Sciacca.

Near Cattolica Eraclea are the interesting remains of a Sicanian town, afterwards colonised by the Phœnicians and called Heracleia Minoa by the Greeks.

Girgenti or Akragas ranked with Syracuse as one of the principal centres of Greek culture in Sicily ; it was unsurpassed for the number and beauty of its temples

Phalaris, Tyrant

and their magnificent position. The modern town is picturesquely situated on a hill, which extending from west to east, terminates in the Rupe Atenea, on whose summit stood the temple of Athena. From this point a marvellous view is enjoyed of mountains, valleys, plain and sea ; in the foreground stretches the low green hill with its group of glorious temples, famous as those of Athens itself.

Legend traces the foundation of this city to Dædalus, possibly because the first colonists came in 582 B.C. from Gela, which had been founded by Dorians from Crete and Rhodes. The new city was named Akragas and stood within the triangle formed by the long ridge of Monte Camico on which the modern town stands, and the two rivers Akragas and Drago, now San Biagio and Sant' Anna, which meet in a common estuary. The southern-most point was probably the hill on which the temples stand.

Three names are prominent in the history of Akragas : Phalaris, Theron and Empedocles.

Phalaris, a ferocious tyrant, ruled the city from 565 to 549 B.C. Among his other enormities he offered human sacrifices to Moloch the Punic God, roasting his enemies alive in the hollow body of a bronze bull. Popular vengeance overtook him and a few years later arose Theron (488–472), a mild and benevolent tyrant under whose rule Akragas became prosperous and extended her territory to the river Himera, where Theron and his son-in-law, Gelon of Syracuse, won the famous victory over the Carthaginians in 480. He fortified the city, and most of the temples were built during his reign. Pindar in his Odes celebrated the generosity and benevolence of Theron and his victories in the Olympic Games.

A TOMB-DWELLING AT SYRACUSE

The goatherd, his family and live stock, all live happily in this rock-hewn
Greek tomb, undisturbed by the ghosts of its former occupants.

Empedocles

Pindar refers to the city of Akragas as "incredibly opulent and the most beautiful city of mortals." At one time it numbered 200,000 inhabitants. It was rich in commerce and its inhabitants devoted themselves to art and pleasure, the luxury of their banquets and the magnificence of their hospitality being renowned.

Empedocles, that versatile genius, was born in Akragas ; during Theron's reign and the Republic which followed he devoted his manifold talents to the good of his fellow countrymen. Poet, philosopher and scientist, his skill in healing disease was such as to earn for him the reputation of a magician, and his eccentric mode of dress and life lent colour to the supposition. He was adored by the people and statues were raised to him during his lifetime. To him is attributed the making of an artificial gap in Monte Camico, where the Prefecture now stands, in order to let the healthy north wind blow through and disperse the malaria of the plain.

Empedocles' death was as strange as his life. He is said to have thrown himself into the crater of Etna so that men might think he had vanished like a God ; but shortly afterwards the volcano threw up one of his well-known sandals and thus proclaimed the manner of his death !

Akragas remained neutral in the war between Athens and Syracuse, caring more for art and luxury than for arms, but was betrayed to the Carthaginians in 406, when Himilcon plundered it and set fire to the temples. Restored by Timoleon it finally passed in 262 to the Romans, who changed its name to Agrigentum. The Saracens took it in A.D. 827, naming it Gergent, and Girgenti it remained until 1927, when the National Government decreed the restoration of its Roman name, and the City of Many Temples once more became Agrigento.

When planning a tour in Sicily travellers seldom realise how much there is to see at Girgenti or how great are the distances between the various points of interest. The usual two days are wholly inadequate and leave only a confused memory of splendid ruins, marred by a sense of hurry and fatigue. Several days or a week should be devoted to Girgenti, and even this is all too short a time for those to whom classical remains make a strong appeal. Besides, it is a good centre for excursions and a supremely beautiful spot wherein to dream and call up visions of the past.

The beauty of these sublime temples is enhanced by their marvellous setting. Once again the eye is impressed by the gold and green of the Sicilian landscape. These southern hills are clad in every shade of green : pale almond trees, soft olives, orange and lemon groves. Yellow earth and sandstone cliffs crop out from emerald grass, and the temples, rising amid all this greenery, glow like burnished gold in the sunlight.

Accustomed as we are to the golden-brown complexion of the temples of Sicily and Pæstum, we find it difficult to picture them glittering with white and coloured stucco in the time of their glory.

Away to the left and on the highest point of the ridge stands the great Temple of Hera, or Juno Lacinia, built early in the Vth century B.C. Very picturesque it is, though only twenty-five of its thirty-four columns are standing ; most of those on the south side have fallen, corroded by the sirocco which beats mercilessly on this exposed spot. The temple suffered severely in the conflagration of 406 B.C. and the cella still shows traces of fire ; later it was badly damaged by an earthquake.

Temple of Heracles

On a platform to the east stood the sacrificial altar. This temple is said to have contained a painting of Helen by Zeuxis.

The Temple of Concord, built a few years later than that of Juno, is one of the best preserved Doric temples in existence. All its thirty-four fluted columns are standing, with entablature and tympanum complete; only the roof has fallen; the stairs leading to the architrave are still practicable. The cella is reached by a flight of steps.

This exquisite temple suffered less than its companions in the Carthaginian invasion, though even here traces of fire are visible. Its later preservation may be gratefully attributed to the Bishop of Agrigentum, San Gregorio delle Rape, who in A.D. 462 consecrated it as a Christian church. It is true that he built walls and arches in the cella, thus transforming it into a basilica with three naves, but he and his successors protected the building from destruction and it was the cathedral of Girgenti until 1748, when it was restored to its primitive form and declared a national monument. The temple was arbitrarily named " Concord " by Fazello from a Latin inscription found within the precincts, but it is not known to which deity it was dedicated.

Next we come to the Temple of Heracles, until a few years ago a mass of ruins showing evident traces of fire. In 1922 eight of the fallen columns were raised to their original position and the temple, which, according to Cicero, was one of the earliest in Sicily and stood near the Forum, now presents a picturesque outline.

This temple contained a famous painting by Zeuxis of Alcmene and Heracles in his cradle strangling the serpents, and a fine bronze statue of the Demigod which Verres with his usual cupidity tried to steal by night.

Castor & Pollux

His slaves were repulsed by the citizens, who after this attempt guarded their temples continually.

Near the Temple of Heracles are the colossal ruins of the Temple of Zeus, which, after that of Artemis at Ephesus, was the largest Greek temple ever built. So gigantic were the columns of this immense sanctuary that a man could stand in each of their flutings!

The temple was begun in 480 B.C., after the victory of Himera, and was largely built by Carthaginian prisoners. It was still unfinished in 406 B.C. when the Carthaginian invasion put a stop forever to its building. Later wars, earthquakes, devastations of all sorts, threw it completely into ruin. As if this were not enough, great blocks were taken by sacrilegious hands in the reign of Charles V to build the mole at Porto Empedocle!

This huge ruined temple possesses several features unique in Greek art, among them one which links it with the colossal monuments of Egypt. Some part of it, probably the interior entablature, was supported by twelve caryatides and telamones, each measuring twenty-five feet in height. The last three of these fell in 1401, when they were adopted as the arms of the city. One of these giants, reconstructed from eighteen pieces, lies prone among the flowers in the temple precincts. Another peculiarity of this great temple is that it faced west.

At the far corner of a flowery meadow, on the edge of a deep gorge full of lemon trees, stand four graceful columns with their cornice, familiar in all pictures of Girgenti. They belong to the small temple of Castor and Pollux, and were raised and put together in the XIXth century. Close examination shows that they have Roman capitals and probably belonged to two different buildings, but the fragment is one of the most picturesque

Temple of Æsculapius

objects in the Girgenti landscape. The temple has only been partially excavated; in March 1927 two altars were brought to light beyond the columns; one, of circular form, divided into four sections for the simultaneous sacrifice of four animals, is unique among Grecian remains, the only other altar of the same kind hitherto found being a much smaller one at Athens.

Down in the gorge are the remains of the Piscina of Theron and an aqueduct which we can cross with care, ascending then by a rough path to the left. Here beyond the railway we find two columns half built into a farmhouse; these belong to the still buried Temple of Hephæstus or Vulcan.

A road passes between the temples of Heracles and Concord, and leads through the Porta Aurea to the so-called Tomb of Theron, a square building evidently of a later date and too simple to have been the sepulchre of that magnificent ruler. It has also been called the Tomb of Timoleon, or even of a horse, the winner of some famous race. This is quite possible, for we read that the maidens of Girgenti built tombs to their favourite song birds, and this tenderness on the part of the daughters of the luxurious pleasure city towards their little feathered companions strikes an answering chord in the hearts of all animal lovers.

Following the level road for a short distance between fields we come upon the remains of a lonely temple, that of Æsculapius, which until a few years ago was almost hidden by a farmhouse built into its walls. This has now been demolished and the ruins of a small temple *in antis* are exposed to view. This temple was called by Cicero *famosissimum fanum* and possessed a fine statue of Apollo which Verres attempted to steal.

On the hill-side below the Rupe Atenea are the remains

Mosaic Pavements

of yet another temple, the most ancient of them all, dedicated to Demeter and Persephone. The Norman church of San Biagio was built over it and only part of the basement and wall can now be seen; two altars stand between it and the overhanging rock.

On the road leading from the modern town to the temples are the remains of a Græco-Roman house with mosaic pavements. A little further on the right is the XIIIth-century church of San Nicola, whose sandstone façade and graceful Norman portal invite us to enter. The interior is small and plain, with a curious frescoed arcade at the east end. The church seems to have been built on the site of a temple. In the garden behind it is the so-called Oratory of Phalaris, a chapel built on the foundations of a small temple or tomb.

A remarkable feature of Girgenti is its goats. These animals with their satyr-like countenances and musky odour are to be met with everywhere in Sicily and seem to fit in with the landscape; but the goats of Girgenti are a race apart, larger, silkier than those of other places, with broad, twisted horns and aristocratic airs. Majestically, attended by a man on horseback, they stalk in herds along the country roads, or singly, bend their comely heads to crop the flowery grass among the temples.

Here, thanks to the southern peasant's keen sense of the picturesque and equally keen appreciation of its appeal to *moneta*-dispensing foreigners, many a charming tableau presents itself to brush or camera. Near the Temple of Castor and Pollux an aged crone, her silvery locks escaping from a yellow kerchief, may often be seen seated among the ruins, while her grandson, an elfish boy with beady black eyes, leads a milk-white nanny and her curly offspring to graze at the base of the columns. On the appearance of tourists armed with

Museum

Kodaks the animals seem instinctively to pose themselves in graceful attitudes, and *soldi* rain into Beppino's small brown paw.

It is not unusual at a turn in the road to come upon a mother goat proudly surveying her latest achievement—a pair of tiny, fluffy kids, barely half an hour old, already staggering on long, weak legs and blinking in the sunlight which they behold for the first time!

The modern town on the hill consists of one main street, the Via Atenea, narrow and winding, with numerous steep alleys branching off to right and left. One of these on the right leads to the small ruined basilica of Santa Maria dei Greci, built on the site of a temple whose foundations with portions of fluted columns are still visible. Near this is the XIVth-century cathedral of San Gerlando, which has a fine *campanile* with graceful windows. In the sacristy is a rich collection of jewelled and embroidered vestments, reminding us that the bishopric of Girgenti, founded in 1086 by Count Roger, is said to be the richest in Sicily. Another treasure preserved in the Chapterhouse adjoining the cathedral is a wonderful Greek sarcophagus in creamy marble, whereon are carved in high relief and with a delicacy worthy of Praxitiles, four episodes from the story of Phædra and Hippolytus.

The church and convent of Santo Spirito, formerly closed, may now be visited and possess some very beautiful doors and windows, which are shown with wondering pride by the simple-minded nuns, who think it strange that *forestieri* should take the trouble to come and see anything so dilapidated!

The small Museum contains interesting objects found in the neighbourhood; it is well supplemented by the private museum of Baron Gaspare Giudice with its

Benefactors & Enthusiasts

wonderful collection of Greek vases and Siculian pottery. Professor Giuliani and Signor Cesare De Angelis have also interesting collections which they are courteously willing to show to visitors.

There are two other prominent figures so closely connected with Girgenti and its temples that we must mention them here. Commendatore Alexander Hardcastle, an Englishman, came to Girgenti some years ago in search of health and made his home there, becoming the benefactor of the town and the financier of excavations for which the archæological world owes him a debt of gratitude. He it was who caused the columns of the Temple of Heracles to be raised in 1922, and not a month passes but some fresh item is added to the list of his munificence towards the city of his adoption. He bought a villa near the temples, in order to be in touch with what had become his main interest in life.

The Custodian Arancio, a cultured and disinterested classical enthusiast, has for years spent his life among the temples, gladly placing his stores of knowledge at the disposal of all who really care for the lore of ancient Greece. Fortunate are those travellers who have had the privilege of wandering from temple to temple under his guidance, and listening while he quoted Homer's rolling verses in his musical tones or expounded his own particular theories, the result of long and loving study, concerning some disputed point of Pagan symbolism or architectural identity.

The novelist and playwright Luigi Pirandello is a native of Girgenti.

CHAPTER VII

SYRACUSE, although much further south than Palermo, lacks the glowing colours and Oriental scents of La Felice—that Eastern savour which renders the City of Palm Trees so fascinating. Archæologically, however, it is more interesting, for its marvellous ruins speak of the golden days of Greek rule when Syracuse was the flourishing capital of Sicily.

The Greek colony of Syracuse was founded in 734 B.C. by Archias the Corinthian, on the site of a Siculian or perhaps Phœnician city. The name Siracusa is derived either from a Phœnician word meaning *eastern* or from the neighbouring swamp Syraka. Ortigia was so named by the Greeks from the sacred forest of Artemis at Ephesus, and they built there the first temple to the goddess in Sicily.

Legend relates that Archias, a rich Heraclid of Corinth, had stained his hands with human blood ; fearing the wrath of the gods he consulted the oracle at Delphi and was told to " cross the sea and found a Corinthian colony in that island where Alphæus mingles his waters with the fair Arethusa." And so he came to Sicily, to the island Ortigia, where the river-god Alphæus had rushed in headlong passion to seize the beautiful nymph, who was changed by Artemis into a fountain, and the two plunged underground, passing under the sea to Elis.

The colony grew rapidly into a flourishing city, and only seventy years after its foundation it was able to

Hiero

found two colonies : Acre, now Palazzolo Acreide, and Enna, or Castrogiovanni.

Syracuse was at first a republic, but in 485 B.C., owing to the struggles between nobles and people, Gelon, tyrant of Gela, extended his sway to Syracuse and made it his capital. Under him the city became rich and powerful, rivalling Athens and Alexandria and numbering about 200,000 inhabitants. Gelon defeated the Carthaginians at Himera in 480 and imposed upon them among his conditions of peace that they should cease sacrificing human victims to Poseidon and their other gods.

The Golden Age of Greek supremacy in Sicily now began and for many years the fortunes of the island were bound up with those of Syracuse. Gelon was revered after his death as a demigod, and was succeeded by Hiero I, at whose court Æschylus, Pindar, Simonides, Bacchylides, Pausanias and Epicharmus found a welcome. Hiero was three times victorious at the Olympic Games and Pindar dedicated four odes to him.

In 415 the Athenians, summoned to help the Segestans, sent a fleet under Nicias to conquer Syracuse. The city was reduced to great straits, for the enemy stormed the heights of Epipolæ and nearly surrounded it by a double wall, but at last fortune favoured the Syracusans, and with the help of the Spartans, led by Gylippus, the Athenians were defeated in a great naval battle and again on land, and Demosthenes and Nicias were forced to surrender with all their men (413). It was on this occasion that 7000 Athenian prisoners were confined in the Latomie or quarries, where the greater part of them languished and died, while some were sold as slaves and a fortunate few earned their liberty by reciting the verses of Euripides. It is said that on obtaining their freedom these survivors of one of the greatest horrors in history

Dionysius

hurried to Athens and threw themselves at the feet of the poet whose genius had been instrumental in saving their lives.

In 405 Dionysius I, who had risen from scribe to general, became tyrant of Syracuse and reigned for thirty-seven years ; he defeated the Carthaginians under Himilcon, ruled over the greater part of Sicily and Magna Græcia, and was considered next in power to the King of Persia.

Dionysius is one of the picturesque figures of Syracusan history, and round his complex personality many legends have collected. He was undoubtedly a great military genius and the saviour of Hellenism in Sicily, for he stemmed the overwhelming tide of Carthaginian invasion. He built the great wall of Epipolæ, more than three miles in length, in twenty days, employing 60,000 free men to whom he paid double wages, and superintending the work himself. The huge blocks used were taken from the Latomie. He enriched his navy with two hundred new ships, refitted a hundred and ten old ones, caused 140,000 shields, a corresponding number of swords and helmets, and 14,000 cuirasses to be made. During his reign long-range catapults were introduced ; those previously in use could only hurl stones 600 feet. He also launched the first ship with five banks of oars, and one of these vessels, richly decorated, brought from Locri one of the two brides whom he married on the same day, and with whom he seems to have lived happily.

This many-sided ruler was moreover a patron of the arts and aspired to be something of a poet himself. Plato and other great men were welcome visitors at his court. His life, like that of many other tyrants, was embittered by the dread of assassination, and many stories are told of his exaggerated precautions to ensure safety. This fear no doubt gave rise to the actions which have procured for him a reputation for cruelty, belied by certain acts of clemency. One incident shows a mode of reasoning akin to the Freudian theory of the " unconscious wish " ! A favourite guard of Dionysius was unwise enough not only to dream that he had murdered his master, but also to tell his dream. Dionysius ordered his immediate execution, saying that " before dreaming of such a crime he must often have thought of committing it ! "

Strange to say, this tyrant died, not by assassination, but from excess of joy over the successful performance in Greece of a play he had written !

Syracuse continued to prosper under her tyrants until Hieronymus allied himself with the Carthaginians and thus drew upon his city the wrath of Rome. It was taken in 212 by Marcellus and reduced to the condition of a Roman provincial town. In A.D. 535 it was conquered by Belisarius and for a brief period became the seat of Government of the Byzantine Empire, but it was destroyed by the Saracens in 878 and never recovered. Count Roger took it in 1085, but he and his successors made Palermo their capital and Syracuse was henceforward left to dream among the ruins of the glorious past and has no mediæval or modern history. A few handsome Norman and Spanish buildings in the so-called modern town testify to the passage of these later conquerors, but the city has remained wholly Greek, one fancies even in the character of the inhabitants, who are more curious and talkative than the Palermitans and lack the touch of Oriental aloofness which distinguishes the latter.

The city was originally divided into five quarters

which are still distinctly traceable : Epipolæ, Tyche, Neapolis and Achradina on the mainland, and the island of Ortigia connected with it by a causeway. Ortigia is apt to be somewhat neglected by tourists who, having little time at their disposal, prefer to spend it among the splendid ruins on the mainland. But a prolonged sojourn in the small island town, with leisure for strolling through its crooked streets, leads to many interesting discoveries. The irregular lines of huddled, nondescript houses are here and there broken by a lordly Norman façade or a pretentious Spanish balcony. One comes upon elaborate doorways, built up arches with richly carved keystones, exquisite windows, strange gargoyle heads at street corners, while the balcony supports in carved stone or marble are a study in themselves. A remarkable example in the Via Gelone consists of four prominently carved heads, part animal, part grotesquely human, on which the balcony rests ; while on the arched doorway beneath a relief of the sacred monstrance is in strange contrast with those diabolical faces which grin down upon it.

At a corner of the Via Roma is a curiosity of a different kind : a tabernacle containing a painted Madonna, around which hang many plaits of hair, fair, brown and black ! The nearness of one of the barbers' shops which abound in Ortigia perhaps accounts for these uncommon votive offerings.

The house doors in the narrow streets often open straight into well-furnished bedrooms and the people seem for the most part prosperous and independent. Adult beggars are rare, but among the children, even when quite well dressed, the habit of asking for *moneta* is prevalent, much as the children of Siena clamour for stamps.

Temple of Apollo

The names of many of the old streets and alleys are significant : Via Pegaso, Vicolo Caronte, Ronco Pirro, etc. (*Ronco* means blind alley, of which there are many in this quaint old town.)

Some of the earliest Greek remains in Syracuse are to be found in Ortigia, as for instance the Temple of Apollo, whose broken columns are protected by a railing in the Via Diana. It is ten feet below the street level and is overlooked by picturesquely untidy houses, whose inhabitants, familiarised by long custom, scarcely glance at the wonderful ruin under their windows, except when foreigners, who interest them greatly, are seen poking about among the moss-grown foundations.

Twenty glorious Doric columns are all that remain of the Vth-century Temple of Athena, and until a few years ago they were built up in the walls of the present cathedral, Santa Maria del Piliero. They have now been uncovered and are a source of joy to all lovers of classical beauty. Looking down the south aisle in the mellow evening light, the long line of these fluted columns, severely simple, is wholly satisfying to the eye. They were originally thirty-six and the temple to which they belonged was about the same size as that of Neptune at Pæstum. The font is a large marble Greek vase of exquisite form, supported by seven mediæval bronze lions. The temple was converted into a Christian church in 640 A.D. ; it became a mosque in 878, and possesses Saracenic battlements.

Close to this temple stood a smaller and older one also dedicated to Athena. It was of the VIIth century B.C. and the population evidently outgrew it and built the larger one by its side. This little gem, rich in coloured decoration, was discovered in 1914, during the asphalting of the Via Minerva, and, sad to say, it was

The Olympeium

sacrificed to the exigencies of road-making. All its more important parts are, however, preserved in the Museum, opposite the cathedral.

Here are many interesting relics of Syracusan history ranging from the earliest specimens of Sicanian pottery and the contents of Siculian tombs at Megara Iblea, to an exquisite statue of Aphrodite of the late Praxitelian school found by Marchese Landolina in the Bonavia garden in 1804. The head and one arm are missing, but even thus mutilated, the statue is very lovely. The Museum also possesses a fine collection of coins.

At the southernmost extremity of Ortigia stands the Castello Maniace, guarding the narrow entrance to the Porto Grande. It was built by the Byzantine general, Giorgio Maniaces, on the site of a temple of Hera and added to in succeeding centuries. The fine Gothic entrance gate and a few rooms and passages are all that remain of the once impregnable fortress, but the view from the bastions, especially at sunset, should not be missed.

The Porta Marina, a fine Spanish XVth-century structure, stands at the entrance to the Passeggiata Aretusa, a broad tree-shaded avenue facing the Porto Grande. This is the favourite promenade of the Syracusans. Close by in the harbour the steamers plying to Tripoli and Malta ride at anchor ; and when the fleet is cruising in Sicilian waters a row of destroyers may often be seen moored to the quay.

Across the sparkling blue waters of the Porto Grande the eye rests on the long purple chain of the Hyblean Mountains, while on the foreshore at their foot rise two tall columns, all that are left of the famous Olympeium or temple of Olympian Zeus, for whose statue Gelon gave a golden robe from the spoils of Himera and

The Fount of Arethusa

Dionysius I sacrilegiously removed it, saying that it was "too cold in winter and too heavy in summer!"

A visit to these lonely columns may be combined with a trip up the Ciane river, often confused with the Anapo, whose course is for some distance parallel to it. This is a most enjoyable excursion occupying three or four hours. We sail across the Porto Grande and row up the narrow stream, which in its higher reaches is thickly bordered by papyrus, the plants in some places reaching a height of twenty feet. Very picturesque they are, their graceful feathery tufts swaying in the breeze. The boatman cuts one down and slicing the stem with his knife produces long strips of white pith—the "paper" which when dried can be used for writing or painting. Several of these strips, welded and pressed together, form the cards sold in Syracuse with paintings of Sicilian carts and local costumes. This is the only place in Europe where the papyrus grows wild; it was introduced by the Saracens.

At length we reach a deep dark pool, called Testa della Pisma, in which the "azure spring" Ciane wells up unceasingly. Stories are told of a submerged castle and a shadowy figure which at midday flits across the blue depths. The banks are studded with flowers; jewelled dragonflies swoop and flash over the still pool; and in the hush of midday enchantment one is ready to believe anything, for is not this the haunt of the nymph, Persephone's companion, who was changed by Hades into a spring for opposing his will?

Returning to Ortigia, we pause beside the Fountain of Arethusa the watery haunt of that other nymph, whose semicircular marble basin is also shaded by papyrus. Water fowl rock on the surface, fish dart swiftly among the shadows. The water is now brackish, but as

GREEK THEATRE, SYRACUSE

This theatre, the largest of the ancient world, can seat more than 10,000 spectators. In the distance
Ortigia stands out white against the blue Ionian Sea.

recently as 1798 it must have been fresh and pure, for Nelson watered his fleet at this spring.

Close by in a small and well-kept garden is the statue of Archimedes, that great son of Syracuse who benefited his country by many inventions, and with his burning glass set fire to the enemy ships in the harbour. It is said that, intent on a geometrical drawing in the sand, he sharply reproved a rough soldier of Marcellus who had stepped on it and who, in ignorant irritation, drew his sword and slew the great man whom his chief had given orders to spare.

Syracuse, like all other Sicilian cities, has its own peculiar Easter ceremonies. On Holy Thursday each church has its Sepulchre, and crowds of people move slowly from one to another till late in the evening. At Santo Spirito the whole choir is transformed into a stage with scenery, where a group of life-sized painted wooden figures represents Christ bearing the cross, attended by two negroes, with the Madonna, St. John and Magdalen on the right and Roman soldiers on the left. This group, brilliantly lighted, is very impressive.

On Holy Thursday and Good Friday numbers of small children may be seen in the streets dressed as little priests, tiny angels with elaborate paper wings, mourners with long black veils and so forth. They are in readiness for the Good Friday procession which, lighted by hundreds of tapers, parades the principal streets as soon as it is dark.

First come the various guilds with their banners, marching to the accompaniment of muffled drums. Next follow women in mourning veils and the little dressed-up children, some of the smallest already asleep in their fathers' arms. Then a life-sized Madonna in deepest black is carried aloft and a glass and gilt

casket follows in which lies the dead Christ. The mitred
Archbishop and his clergy are close behind and the
band brings up the rear, the mournful strains of the
" Miserere " from *Il Trovatore* wailing out upon the still
night air and followed by " Ah che le morte," taken
cheerfully in valse time ! A truly southern touch which
anywhere but in Italy would seem incongruous !

.   .   .   .   .

Crossing to the mainland by the bridge we pass through
extensive suburbs where new buildings are rapidly
springing up. In the bare and dusty Piazza del Foro a
railing protects a row of column bases and one erect
column of red marble, part of the ancient Agora, and
we wonder how many more of these remains lie buried
under our feet. No doubt the building operations in
progress all over this area will bring to light much that is
of interest.

A more enjoyable and less dusty way of reaching
Achradina is by the ferry across the Porto Piccolo,
which lands us in the suburb of Santa Lucia, near the
church of the same name. This Norman building stands
on the site of the Virgin's martyrdom ; she is the
Patroness of Syracuse and her statue by Gagini is in the
cathedral ; her body, which originally rested in a crypt
beneath the church dedicated to her, was removed by
Giorgio Maniaces and is now in Venice.

In this same neighbourhood is the church of San
Giovanni and the entrance to extensive catacombs, of
which there are many in this district ; Syracuse ranks
next to Rome in the number of these subterranean
labyrinths. The Catacombs of San Giovanni are enor-
mous and only partially explored. They are of later date
than any of the others (IVth to VIth century A.D.). Close

Latomia dei Cappuccini

by are the remains of an ancient basilica with three
naves, once the cathedral of Syracuse, under which is the
crypt of San Marziano, where St. Paul is believed to have
preached during his three days' sojourn in the city.

The world-famous Latomia dei Cappuccini in the
garden of the Hotel Villa Politi is near here, and fortunate
are those visitors who can secure rooms in this much-
frequented hotel, which stands in the midst of all these
archæological treasures.

It is impossible to describe the charm of this beautiful
Latomia, so vast that it is easy to lose one's way amid
the winding paths where roses, bougainvillea, hibiscus
and every kind of luxuriant vegetation run riot—its
atmosphere must be felt. Down in this deep quarry whose
walls of rock rise up sheer for 100 feet, where on sultry
afternoons not a leaf stirs and the heady perfume of
lemon blossom hangs almost tangibly on the still air, we
seem cut off from the upper world and enfolded in a
dream of the past.

The ghosts of the 7000 Athenians return to people the
scene of their sufferings ; shrubs, creepers and flowers
fade away and there is nothing but pitiless rock under
a pitiless sky. Bearded veterans, splendid youths such
as Praxiteles loved to model, stagger about delirious with
thirst, stumbling over the bodies of their dead and dying
comrades ; many fall and are too weak to rise again.
Under the shadow of a grotto a young man has collected
a group of fellow prisoners and is endeavouring to make
them forget their sufferings for an hour by reciting
passages from Euripides in a slow, musical voice. The
golden verses flow melodiously from his parched lips ;
his listeners are transported to the cool glades and
bubbling fountains of their own land. One, a mere boy,
worn by privation and disease, reclines against the rocky

99

wall, gazing with wrapt attention at the reciter's face. Gradually his head droops lower, his eyes close, with a sigh he sinks to the ground. The reciter breaks off short in the middle of a verse, springs to his friend's side and bending over him, calls him by name ; but there is no response, for the weary spirit has left its prison and flown away on the wings of divine poetry, leaving only an inanimate body lying in the Latomia, a smile on the upturned face. . . .

A sudden chill disperses the vision—the sun is gone, evening has fallen, and with almost a sense of fear we make our way to the steps and climb out of the haunted spot.

In the Neapolis quarter is the small Latomia of Santa Venera, now a charming garden, and the Latomia del Paradiso, interesting because it contains the Orecchio di Dionisio, an artificial grotto in the form of an ear and possessing extraordinary acoustic properties, the slightest sound being loudly reproduced in the depths of the cavern 200 feet away. Legend attributes this ingenious construction to Dionysius I, saying that with his usual fear of conspiracy, he had it made so as to overhear from a small upper chamber all that was whispered by the prisoners below. It appears, however, that the grotto received its name and the legend originated in 1586 when the painter Caravaggio and the archæologist Mirabella visited it together.

Close to the Orecchio di Dionisio is the Grotta dei Cordari, a curious pillared cave which for centuries has been used as a rope-walk. The garden in the Latomia del Paradiso occupies the large central space and enclosed by a wall, which somewhat detracts from its picturesqueness, but it is luxuriant with flowers.

Neapolis is rich in imposing ruins. An immense

The Greek Theatre

Amphitheatre built in the reign of Augustus by Sicilian workmen is one of the most perfect in existence and little inferior in size to that of Verona. Near it stands the small Norman church of San Nicolò where the funeral of Jourdain, son of Count Roger, was held in 1093. Under the church is the Piscina, a reservoir which communicated by a canal with the Amphitheatre.

A little further on is the huge Hecatomb Altar of Hiero II, on which 450 bulls were sacrificed simultaneously to Zeus the Liberator, in commemoration of the expulsion of the tyrant Thrasybulus in 466.

And now we come to the Greek Theatre, the largest of the ancient world and the pride of Syracuse. It is hewn out of the rocky hill-side and was probably constructed by Hiero I (478–467 B.C.), added to by Hiero II and later by the Romans. The pavement of the orchestra and the first eleven rows of seats were at one time covered with marble. Very little of the stage remains, but the semicircle of the auditorium is complete and from the topmost gallery there is a magnificent view of the city, the harbour, and Cape Plemmirio stretching out into the Ionian Sea.

This is one of the most suggestive monuments of Syracuse and full of memories of the past. Here, on these stone seats, Æschylus, Pindar and Plato sat to witness the performance of some great tragedy. Here *The Persians* of Æschylus was performed to commemorate the victory of Himera. And here, of late years, the revival of Greek Drama in Italy has been initiated. Those who have sat in the great theatre and watched the unfolding of such dramas as *The Seven before Thebes*, *Antigone* and *Medea*, or laughed at the gambols of the merry little Satyrs and the blind fury of the Cyclops, while the sun went slowly down behind the

Links with the Past

Hyblean Mountains, leaving the stage and the vast auditorium in shadow, will never forget the impression produced by those peerless verses, declaimed by Italy's leading actors in those surroundings. To assist at such a scene is to realise something of the part played by these great open-air theatres in the life of the Greek people.

Above the theatre is the Street of the Tombs, whose niches hewn in the rock walls are now empty.

Fort Euryalus in the Epipolæ quarter is the most distant point to be visited and is often omitted for lack of time. But it is intensely interesting and a morning should be devoted to it.

We drive along a country road which winds gradually up hill, passing through cultivated fields and olive groves, then growing bare and stony. At last we reach the great fortress of which, though in ruins, the original plan can be clearly traced. There are the remains of five massive towers, moats and subterranean passages. This fortress was built by Dionysius in 397 for the defence of the city against the Carthaginians. From the walls there is a fine view and within their circuit the grass is bright with flowers.

There are numerous interesting walks in this direction : the line of Dionysius' great wall may be followed and the Scala Greca visited, with several other classic ruins. At the foot of the hill a massive rock-hewn tomb is pointed out as that of Archimedes, though there seems to be no historical foundation for the statement. Wherever we turn we find some link, historical or legendary, with the past, and it is interesting to remember that it was this smiling, fertile country, watched over by distant Etna, and its simple peasant inhabitants, which inspired the exquisite pastoral poetry of Theocritus, the Syracusan.

Photo   *Cutler*

OLD MONASTERY AT SAVOCA NEAR TAORMINA

Savoca, formerly celebrated for its brave inhabitants and rich wine, contains some fine Norman doorways, and the monastery is said to have been founded by St. Anthony of Padua.

CHAPTER VIII

THE HEART OF SICILY

NOTWITHSTANDING a great improvement of late years in roads and railways, a trip into the interior of Sicily is still something of a voyage into the unknown ; one leaves Syracuse or whatever the starting-point may be with a delightful sense of adventure and—if travelling by branch lines—the vaguest idea of when or where one will arrive !

It is advisable on these occasions to limit one's luggage to a light bag or suitcase, for porters (called in Sicilian *paranza,* a word which in other parts of Italy means a fishing-boat) are scarce and at the smaller stations practically non-existent. Consequently an undue amount of luggage hampers one's movements and leads to dialogues like the following :

" What a lot of *bagaglio !* Are you a commercial traveller ? "

" No."

" A shop assistant ? "

" No."

" What are you then ? "

" A journalist."

" Ah . . . *giornalista !* And where are you going to sell all the newspapers you have in those *valigie ?* "

" I don't sell newspapers, I help to write them ! "

" *Per Bacco !* Ciccio, *senti !* D'you hear that ? The *signora* makes newspapers ! Do you print them all yourself with that writing machine ? "

From Syracuse to Ragusa

And so on indefinitely, varied by a minute catechism as to one's age, family, number of children, why travelling alone, etc. If the answer is no children, there are exclamations of surprise and pity, for to be childless or to possess only one or two *bambini* is looked upon by the prolific Sicilians as the greatest of misfortunes.

These conversations are often carried on under difficulties owing to the incomprehensible dialects spoken in some parts of the interior, and the frequent toothlessness of the questioners. In fact as a rule the toothless ones are the most talkative, and they do not always understand Italian. Their readiness to supply the deficiency in porters and their kindness in offering refreshment from the bundles they invariably have with them, make them delightful travelling companions, though one grows rather weary towards the end of a long day of giving one's whole history to every newcomer!

The journey from Syracuse to Ragusa *via* Sortino lies through scenery so weirdly beautiful and unexpected that it is difficult to describe. The line, a marvel of engineering, winds up the gorge of the Anapo, crossing and recrossing the river, which flows over brown stones and describes innumerable curves. The gorge, at first a fertile valley, gradually narrows and the train passes between high cliffs of brown sandstone, adorned with clumps of pink and purple heather, in and out of many short tunnels. Now the vast necropolis of Pantalica appears on the right with its five thousand tombs opening like windows in the sheer face of rock. This is all that remains of an important Siculian city of the XIIth to the VIIth century B.C., where later Byzantine civilisation left its traces. This region has furnished many interesting objects now in the Museum at Syracuse.

Ragusa Ibla

Up and up climbs the little train, puffing its way to the summit of the Hyblean Mountains (2285 feet), where a wide tableland broken by small hills and valleys extends for miles like another world. Here, near the source of the Anapo, is Palazzolo Acreide, the ancient Acre, the first colony founded by the Syracusans in 664 B.C. It possesses a small, well preserved Greek Theatre, where in 1927 classical performances were held in connection with those at Syracuse, an adjoining Odeum, Baths and Latomia. All this region is rich in early mosaics.

The line continues to Ragusa (1630 feet), traversing miles of cultivated land divided into fields by stone walls —a curious landscape with a wide horizon. One looks in vain for peasants tilling the fertile soil, and the sight of all those corn and bean fields, so neat and cared for, apparently without human agency, produces a strange, dreamlike impression and recalls the legend that corn first grew in Sicily by spontaneous generation !

At length Ragusa appears, a town of considerable size, spreading over both sides of a chasm spanned by a picturesque bridge. Deep down in the gully are green market gardens flanked by numerous caves and grottoes of Siculian origin. The town itself contains little of interest, but the inhabitants are careful to remind the visitor that it is a " *capoluogo di provincia* " and thus of considerable importance. The large and imposing church standing above the Piazza is bare except for a gorgeously painted ceiling of green, white and gold. Asphalt is found in the neighbourhood.

Ragusa Ibla or Inferiore, reached by a long flight of steps, is far more interesting and contains several XVth-century churches, the remains of Byzantine walls and some of the best work of the painter Pietro Novelli.

Gela

The inhabitants are ethnically different from those of the upper town, which was founded by exiles from Cosenza.

We may return to Syracuse by the main line, stopping at picturesque Modica to visit the castle, which stands on a height overlooking the city. It was built before the Saracen invasion, on the site of a temple of the Sun; some of the columns belonging to this earlier building may still be seen in the courtyard. Faded portraits of the Grimaldi family hang in the empty rooms. On the face of a tower is an immense clock which still chimes the hours.

This castle was the seat of the Counts of Modica, the first of whom, Gualtiero, was a famous admiral under William the Good. In course of time the countship together with vast domains passed to the powerful Chiaramonte family, whose strongholds we meet with all over Sicily. They came with Count Roger and for centuries held an important share in the government of the island.

Near Modica are the curious Cave d' Ispica with their prehistoric tombs and cave dwellings.

Some miles from the station of Noto is Noto Vecchia, a Siculian city which became important under the Saracens but was completely destroyed by an earthquake in 1693.

The line from Ragusa to Girgenti passes Terranova, which has now resumed its ancient name of Gela. Here are the remains of a Doric temple, probably that of Apollo from which Hamilcar stole the famous statue, found later by Alexander the Great at Tyre. It was at Gela that the poet Æschylus met his death; according to tradition he was wandering in the fields when an eagle, mistaking his bald head for a stone, dropped a tortoise upon it and fractured his skull.

MCNKS AT SAVOCA

These bearded Capuccini enjoy one of the finest views in Sicily. But their hill town can only be reached on foot or muleback.

Naro

The scenery for some distance after leaving Ragusa is bare and cold, but later we cross a fertile plain with the sea on one hand and a long mountain range on the other, and catch a glimpse of picturesque Favara on a hill.

One of the most interesting hill towns of Southern Sicily is Naro, easily reached from Girgenti by rail or road. And it is from Girgenti that the traveller should visit it, not as the present writer unwisely did, from Syracuse, arriving late on a dark and rainy March evening!

Tightly wedged between stout peasants with large bundles in the rickety box on wheels which did duty for a station bus, I was swung round dizzy curves, up and up in the darkness, until the crazy vehicle rattled through a narrow street and came to rest in a dim, unpaved *piazza*. Stepping down stiffly into a deep puddle, I enquired for the Podestà, eager to present the letter which would ensure his hospitable care and a decent lodging. A number of men and boys instantly appeared on the scene, and a heated discussion ensued as to the Podestà's whereabouts; at last I was directed to seek him at the Club across the way.

Great was the surprise of the Club members when a bedraggled stranger burst into their midst enquiring anxiously for the Podestà!

" The Podestà is away."

" The Vice-Podestà, then ? "

" He has gone home to bed. You must call again to-morrow."

" But I must present this letter to-night; it is from Professor Orsi of Syracuse."

" PROFESSOR ORSI ? "

The effect of the great archæologist's name was magical. They looked at each other in awed surprise, then all bowed obsequiously and a tall man stepped forward.

"I am the Podestà's brother-in-law," he said courteously, "in what way can I serve you?"

In a few minutes I was installed in the best room of the *locanda* or inn—a great, cheerless, barn-like chamber containing three beds, a table, two chairs, a chest of drawers and a primitive washstand. The *padrone* was exhorted to bring out his best linen for the distinguished visitor, who was a friend of the great Professor Orsi and the guest of the Municipio. Supper, consisting of soup, eggs, bread, fruit and a bottle of Marsala, was brought from the *trattoria* by "Caruso," a ragged urchin who, to my horror, produced a glass from his dirty pocket and proceeded to pour the Marsala into it! Bewildered by all these extraordinary happenings, I wondered for a moment whether this barefooted boy waiter could be a relation of the great tenor, but quickly realised that *caruso* is the generic name for boys in this part of Sicily.

The host, a kindly, genial personage, somewhat flurried by the unexpected arrival, under the protection of the Podestà's brother-in-law, of a *forestiera*—probably the first who had ever slept under his roof—reiterated his assurances that the sheets were his best and *had not been slept in*, and that, notwithstanding the three beds, the room was entirely at the *signora's* disposal and she might, if she so pleased, lock the door! He then provided such a plentiful supply of really hot water as to put to shame the milk-jug of tepid liquid often offered by more pretentious hotels!

In spite of this hospitable reception, it was an uncomfortable night. The wind, cold and damp, whistled through a broken window-pane. The room was like a vault and not even the weight of blankets and thick quilts from all three beds could warm the unfortunate *forestiera*, who lay shivering between the clean sheets and wishing that Professor Orsi had not advised her to spend the night at Naro !

Next morning the Podestà's brother-in-law, the Vice-Podestà, and various municipal officials devoted themselves to the task of escorting their guest to see the sights of Naro. It was a kind of Royal Progress, the procession gathering volume as it passed through the quaint streets of the little town so justly praised by Professor Orsi, archæologist and Senator of Italy.

Perched on a conical hill, at a height of 1940 feet, Naro dominates the surrounding country, and from its ruined castle the panorama, extending to Etna and Taormina, is superb.

The castle is one of the many Chiaramonte fortresses scattered throughout the island. Two windows in the tower and a fine Norman-Gothic doorway are all that remains of architectural value, but the commanding position and wonderful view make it worth the climb through steep and not over-clean streets.

The town is rich in churches with fine late Norman portals. One, the ancient cathedral near the castle, is disused and in ruins. It is believed to have been built by William the Good about 1200. The beautiful west door, approached by a flight of steps, is unfortunately damaged. The present cathedral contains a square Byzantine font mounted on the stump of a Corinthian column, and two marble groups by Gagini, spoilt by a later application of colour. Santa Caterina, a basilica of fine proportions with traces of frescoes, has recently been restored. In San Francesco are a silver Madonna and two embalmed bodies of saints in rich costumes, reclining in graceful attitudes in glass sarcophagi under

A Kindly Folk

opposite altars. Sant' Agostino possesses a collection of gorgeously embroidered vestments.

A number of vestments, altar frontals and valuable silver ecclesiastical objects are now in the Municipal Museum.

The Palazzo Malfitani has a remarkable corner window with column and cornice, said to be almost unique; in every street of the little town we come upon fine doorways and façades.

The inhabitants of Naro are kindly, hospitable folk, proud of their town and delighted to show it to visitors; they consider its position one of the most beautiful in Sicily. When the richly cultivated land at the foot of the hill is a mass of almond blossom floating above a carpet of emerald green, with the African Sea glittering like silver in the distance and the dark mountains rising peak above peak to the north, it is certainly a typical Sicilian landscape. And the groups of cloaked and hooded men standing in the Piazza, the soft-voiced women in their shawls, the pretty dark-eyed children, make up a picturesque *ensemble* which lingers in the mind long after one has descended to the plain in the rickety motor-bus, and Naro on its hill-top has vanished in the mist.

The most interesting feature of Naro is Il Castellaccio, a prehistoric ruin at some distance from the town, popularly called " La Reggia del Re Cocculo " (a mythical king of the Sicanians about 2000 B.C.). The neighbourhood is honeycombed with grottos and tombs, and Siculian utensils have been found there. Nearer the town are the Grotte Meravigliose, a series of Christian catacombs.

The historian Piccone identifies Naro with Agrigento Ionico; it seems uncertain whether the river Akragas

was the Naro or the San Biagio at Girgenti. Some
derive the name Naro from the Arabic *nare* (fire), as the
arms of the town are three towers surmounted by flames.

Up in the hills to the north of Girgenti is one of the
most interesting of the Chiaramonte castles, Mussomeli.
This fortress was built by the Saracens, as its name testi-
fies ; it rebelled in 860 and was besieged by them. Later
it was rebuilt by Manfredi III Chiaramonte, and became
the largest and most impregnable stronghold in Sicily.

A curious phenomenon met with here and there in the
interior of Sicily is the mud volcano or Macaluba. The
most remarkable of these is within easy reach of Girgenti,
near Aragona-Caldare. It can only be approached on
foot across rough, undulating fields. At one point a
muddy stream must be crossed by stepping-stones and
a low hill climbed, on whose summit a kind of slimy
glitter has been visible from afar. Here we find ourselves
in the midst of a number of miniature craters in which the
salt mud is bubbling and apparently boiling. We dip
a finger gingerly in the mud and discover to our surprise
that it is quite cold ! Its strange behaviour is caused by
the carburetted hydrogen below forcing its way to the
surface. The hill-top is bare and slimy, as nothing will
grow near the craters, but its lower slopes are gay with
flowers, the grape hyacinth growing there in great
profusion and forming large blue patches.

As yet these mud springs have not been exploited, but
the phenomenon is somewhat similar to those of Abano
and Acqui in the north of Italy, where the mud has been
found to be of great medicinal value.

Half-way between Catania and Palermo, in the very
heart of the island, stands Castrogiovanni on its once
impregnable height. It is the " Inespugnabilis Henna "
of Livy, which now, raised to the rank of " capoluogo

The Central Point of Sicily

di provincia," has once more taken its ancient and glorious name.

Enna is one of the most typical and picturesque of Sicilian hill cities, and its many towers have earned for it the title, also applied to Randazzo, of the "San Gimignano of Sicily." As we travel by rail or road through country where richly cultivated zones alternate with arid districts of sulphur mines, the cities of Castrogiovanni and Calascibetta come in sight, crowning twin mountain-tops, each about 3000 feet above sea-level. Their common station is in the valley, and steep roads with sharp curves lead up to the towns, both of which are composed of narrow winding streets. Castrogiovanni is the more interesting of the two, though the view of it from Calascibetta repays a visit to the latter place.

Henna, "l' ombilico della Sicilia," was an ancient Siculian city colonised by Syracuse and the centre of the Demeter and Kore worship in the island. It fell under the tyranny of Dionysius and Agathocles; it was also ruled by Carthage and Rome. Later it was an important Byzantine fortress, besieged in vain by the Saracens in A.D. 851, and only taken by treachery in 859. The Normans, who soon possessed themselves of Calascibetta on the opposite hill, were unable to take Castrogiovanni until 1087. The city was a favourite resort of Frederick II, but suffered much under later rulers. It was one of the first in Sicily to espouse the national cause in 1848 and 1860.

The name Castrogiovanni comes from the Arabic *Casr-Janna*, a corruption of Enna, or from Castrum Hennae. The chief attraction of the town is its marvellous situation and the view from the highest tower of its ruined castle, where a stone is pointed out as the central point of Sicily. From this commanding spot the panorama

AN OLD GATEWAY, TAORMINA
Water carriers at the fountain. The donkey's barrels contain water, as
well as the graceful jars which the women balance on their heads.

The Streets of Enna

is uninterrupted. At our feet are rolling hills and fertile valleys; away to the north we see the whole chain of the Nebrodi and Madonie with their ramifications; several high peaks soaring into the blue are dwarfed by the white majesty of Etna, which appears immense and near, dominating the whole landscape. To the south, half-hidden by green foot-hills, is the Lake of Pergusa, scene of the Rape of Persephone. A cave on its shores is pointed out as the opening through which the Ruler of the Shades passed with his chariot, and the whole countryside is starred with asphodel, the delicate, ill-fated flower which lured the maiden to her doom. Far away through a gap in the hills gleams a silver streak of sea.

The castle, most of whose towers have fallen (it was restored by King Manfred), stands on or near the site of the famous Temple of Demeter, of which nothing remains.

At the opposite end of the town rises a curious octagonal tower in a green enclosure, all that is left of the castle built by Frederick II. In a grassy meadow beyond, a low pillar surmounted by a cross is also said to mark the central point of Sicily, but it is more pleasing to think that the true *ombilico* is at the spot where we feasted our eyes on the glorious view.

Walking through the streets of Enna we come unexpectedly on many fine XVth and XVIth-century façades; the interior of the churches is generally disappointing; whitewash and stucco abound, with here and there an ancient column or pilaster brought, so our guide declares, from the Temple of Demeter. San Biagio possesses two of these columns, evidently Greek; the XIVth-century cathedral has a lovely pilaster and a fine wooden ceiling supported by columns of black alabaster. In Santa Chiara there is an elaborately carved and gilded altar

Two Important Towns

with all its fittings complete and a curious majolica pavement. More beautiful in design is the pavement of San Michele, which bears the date 1762.

The chief architectural peculiarity of the town consists in the numerous *campanili* attached to churches of later date or built into the walls of houses. Some of them have exquisite windows and doorways.

Commercially the two most important towns of the interior are Caltanisetta and Caltagirone, the former being the centre of the sulphur trade and the market for the agricultural produce of the surrounding region, while the latter is noted for its majolica.

Caltanisetta is well situated on a hill and so modern in appearance that the motorist who stops there for lunch on his way from Girgenti to Castrogiovanni is apt to hurry on without realising how much of interest the town contains.

The name Caltanisetta is derived from the Arabic *Kalat* (castle), a common prefix in Sicily, and Nissa, an ancient city which stood on or near the site of the present town. Count Roger drove out the Saracens in 1086 and gave the town to his son Jourdain. He also founded the Abbey of Santo Spirito outside the gates. In this picturesque old church with its great XIVth-century fresco of Christ which recalls the Monreale mosaic, an annual festival is held to commemorate the expulsion of the Angiovins. The church of San Giovanni Battista was also founded by Roger, and that of Santa Maria degli Angeli possesses a fine Norman door.

The castle of Pietrarossa, though restored by him, is of much earlier foundation, Siculian or Roman. It was a massive fortress standing on three rocks united at the base, but in the XVIth century it collapsed suddenly and very little of it is now left.

A Rich Commune

In the church of San Domenico are fifteen extraordinarily life-like groups in wood and *papier mâché*, representing the scenes of the Passion. On Holy Thursday these are carried through the streets lined with devout crowds to the accompaniment of *lamintanze* or mystical laments.

A few miles from Caltanisetta is the Macaluba di Terrapilata, another group of mud volcanoes. Some early ruins in the neighbourhood of Gibilgabbibi are thought to be those of Nissa and Petilia.

Caltagirone, from *kalat* (castle) and *gerun* (grottos), is a picturesque town half-way between Caltanisetta and Syracuse. It stands on three hills, two of which are joined by a fine bridge. Its origin is uncertain ; there is an ancient necropolis of 2000 B.C., and statuettes, vases and coins of many different epochs have been found in the neighbourhood.

Caltagirone was ruled by Byzantines and Saracens ; in 1030 the latter were driven out with the help of the Genoese and the citizens dedicated a church to St. George and added the arms of Genoa, a red cross on a white field, to the spread eagle which already formed the arms of the city. But the Saracens returned and were only finally expelled by Count Roger in 1090, when a church was dedicated to St. James of Compostella in memory of this liberation, and he became Patron of the city.

The fifty feuds occupying two-thirds of the Plain of Catania were granted to Caltagirone by Roger in recognition of help given in the sacking of Zotica, a stronghold of robbers, and this patrimony still makes Caltagirone one of the richest communes of Italy.

In 1542 the city was destroyed by an earthquake and rebuilt at the expense of the Senate ; it was again

Majolica Industry

devastated in 1693 and again restored, so that most of the treasures of early art which it possessed have been lost. Two important exceptions are the Byzantine Madonna di Conadomini in a massive silver frame and a beautiful statue of the Madonna and Child, attributed to Laurana, the father of Sicilian sculpture. These are in the ex-Matrice church. A few pictures and several statues by the Gagini are preserved in other churches.

We have a good opportunity of studying the XIXth-century painter, Francesco Vaccaro, in Caltagirone, his birthplace. This fine but neglected painter is the leading representative of the later Sicilian School. His canvases, full of delicacy and profound religious feeling, are scattered over the island, but few of them have reached the mainland (we only recall one example, Christ bearing the cross, at Naples), and his name is scarcely mentioned in the standard books on Italian painting. The cathedral of Caltagirone is full of his work and a lovely Madonna and Child may be seen in the Museum.

Don Luigi Sturzo, the priest-politician who made such a stir in Italy a few years ago and whose remarkable physiognomy is still the joy of caricaturists, is a native of Caltagirone.

The majolica industry of Caltagirone dates back to Saracen times ; it reached its zenith in the XVIIth and XVIIIth centuries. The modern makers wisely repeat the old designs and rich colouring. Small, artistic terracotta statuettes in peasant costume have also been made here from the middle of last century, and very quaint and charming they are.

A long and wide flight of steps constructed in 1600 leads from the Corso Amedeo to several churches and the ancient walls, from which there is a magnificent view of the surrounding country. On the 25th of July the

Photo　　　　　　　　　　　　　　　　　　　　　*Cutler*

SICILIAN BOYS OF THE INTERIOR

These " carusi " are enjoying life in the sunshine. The shawl is typical
and does not imply a sore throat !

People & Costumes

Scala is brilliantly illuminated and all the peasants of the surrounding countryside flock in their picturesque costumes to watch the procession. These occasions of seeing the people in their national costume are becoming rare in Sicily as elsewhere, though in the deserted roads of the interior we may come upon cloaked and hooded figures mounted on mules, sometimes with the wife riding pillion, and followed by a miscellaneous collection of domestic animals—goats, sheep, pigs, sometimes a small donkey, a cow and one or two dogs—all taking their walk together in perfect harmony! One sees comparatively few men on foot in the country; they usually live in towns and villages far from the fields where they work, and none is so poor but he possesses a mule or donkey on which to ride at a slow and stately pace. The older men often wear knee breeches and leggings, with a cap which droops like a bag over one ear, accentuating the hawk-like expression of the thin, keen-eyed face.

CHAPTER IX

DONNA CICCIA, the *scambio* or charwoman, stumped heavily up the stairs and entered the kitchen of the small flat, from whose window her English employer, wrapped in a fur coat, was gazing in ecstasy at Mount Etna glowing in all the glory of sunrise.

With a curt " *Buon giorno* " and never a glance at the daily miracle which dragged the eccentric *signora* out of bed a few minutes earlier each morning, Donna Ciccia set about lighting the fire. Presently, out of the depths of her puzzled thoughts she spoke :

" *Signora*, why do you get up so early these cold mornings ? It's not yet seven o'clock, but no matter how early I come you are always at the window ! "

" I get up to see the sun rise."

" But have you not the sun there where you live ? "

" Yes, of course we have the sun, but we have no Etna."

" No *Etina* ! But then, if you have not an *Etina*, what is it that brings the cold weather ? "

The peasants of Etna Land cannot imagine a world where their mountain does not reign supreme !

Catania lies in the fertile plain between Etna and the Ionian Sea ; it is dominated by the great mountain whose eruptions have repeatedly destroyed it ; there were three in prehistoric times and history records six ; but after each disaster the inhabitants have patiently rebuilt their city and the present fertility of the soil is due to the many strata of ancient lava below.

Catania

Catania is really the City of Etna; the snowcapped mountain, looming near, is its presiding deity, terrible and benign; the streets are paved with lava and it is largely used in building; the mild climate is kept fresh and healthy by the keen air which blows directly off the snow.

For tourists this city is less interesting than many others, though it has a long history and possesses some archæological remains.

Catania was founded by the Chalcidians about 729 B.C., a few years after Naxos, on the site of a Siculian town. (Legend carries its foundation back to Noah and peoples it with Cyclopes and Læstrygones!) Under the Greeks it was an important city and possessed a famous school of medicine; the poet Stesichorus settled there and died at an advanced age; his tomb is said to have been in the present Piazza Stesicoro. Charondas drew up for Catania a code of laws which was afterwards adopted by all Ionian and Chalcidian colonies in Sicily and Magna Graecia. Hiero I of Syracuse took the town and changed its name to Ætna, but it regained its independence and joined the Athenians in the war against Syracuse. It was conquered by Dionysius and later by the Carthaginians; in 339 Timoleon delivered it from the tyrant Mamercus.

Catania was one of the first Sicilian towns taken by the Romans under Marcellus, who named it Catina and made it one of the most populous cities of the island. It suffered greatly in the civil wars and Augustus sent a new colony to repopulate it. Belisarius took it from the Goths, and in 1071 the Normans ousted the Saracens. Devastated by war and earthquake it passed through many vicissitudes, but has suffered more from the forces of Nature than from the violence of man, its prosperity

An Elephant of Lava

being repeatedly cut short by plague, earthquake or eruption. The terrible eruption of 1669 was followed by the earthquake of 1693, in which 16,000 of the inhabitants perished. After this the city was entirely rebuilt, so that its numerous churches are in baroque style, some of them possessing handsome façades.

St. Peter is said to have visited Catania and consecrated a round church to the Madonna while she was still on earth !

The cathedral, dedicated to the virgin martyr and Patroness of Catania, Sant' Agata, was founded by Count Roger in 1091, but was entirely rebuilt after the earthquake of 1669. The façade by Vaccarini (1736) is of massive proportions and adorned by statues. The granite columns are from the ancient theatre. Within the church is the tomb of the composer Bellini, touching in its simplicity. The carved choir stalls are of 1588 and in the sacristy is an interesting painting by an eyewitness of the eruption of 1669. The chapel of Sant' Agata contains relics of the Saint ; among the treasures is a crown studded with precious stones, said to have been given by Richard Cœur de Lion.

The *festa* of Sant' Agata takes place with an interesting procession on the 5th of February ; her relics are held to be potent in stemming the tide of lava and deviating it from the city, and in times of eruption they are carried in solemn procession to the danger zone.

Beneath the cathedral and extending for some distance under the Piazza are the remains of Roman Baths and tortuous passages.

In the centre of the Piazza stands the famous Elephant, an attractive beast of lava, with trunk extended in a friendly and natural manner ; he bears on his back an Egyptian obelisk of granite, probably from the Roman

The Greek Theatre

Circus of Catania. The elephant is the work of an early sculptor, some say the mythical Dædalus, others the magician Heliodorus, who when condemned to death in Constantinople in the VIIIth century A.D., escaped and flew to Catania. The local name for the elephant is *diottru*, a corruption of Eliodoro.

Following the Via Garibaldi, which starts opposite the cathedral, we come to Piazza Mazzini, a small and picturesque square surrounded by arcades whose marble columns were taken from the ancient basilica. A baroque gateway of 1768 closes the vista of the long street. At the end of the Via Auteri is the Castello Ursino, built by Frederick II as a menace to the rebellious towns-people. Its walls were originally washed by the sea, but in the eruption of 1669 the lava stream flowed round it, isolating it and changing the whole aspect of this part of Catania. Now only the keep remains, an imposing fortress in the midst of a desert of waste ground surrounded by squalid houses.

Returning to Piazza Mazzini we proceed through what was once a district entirely given over to churches and monasteries, and arrive at the most interesting ruin in Catania—the Greek Theatre, where probably Alcibiades harangued the Catanese in 415 B.C. to win them over to the cause of Athens. The theatre was of lava with marble-covered orchestra and could seat 7000 spectators. The superstructure is Roman. Count Roger helped himself ruthlessly to materials from this theatre for the building of the cathedral. Close by is the usual small Odeum, a miniature theatre for musical rehearsals.

Under the church of Santa Maria dell' Indirizzo are extensive remains of a Bathing Establishment. There are some traces of the Roman Forum and in the Piazza

Catania's Famous Men

Stesicoro a part of the Amphitheatre is uncovered; the whole circuit, lighted by electricity, can be followed underground.

The only church of special interest is San Nicolò, which stands at the top of the steep Via Lincoln. It has a curious and massive unfinished façade and is the largest church in Sicily. It possesses an immense organ whose building took twelve years. The builder, Donato del Piano, is buried underneath his masterpiece. Across the transepts a meridian is traced with months and days inscribed, and a hole in the roof is so contrived as to cause a ray of sunshine to rest at each midday on that particular date in the calendar. We enquired what would happen on the 29th of February, which was then approaching but no satisfactory answer was forthcoming! An elaborate tabernacle stands in the centre of a charming cloister garden.

Adjoining the church is a small but interesting Museum, containing a few fine pictures, ancient and modern. One of the latter by Natale Attanasio da Catania (1889), entitled "Sunt lacrimæ rerum," is a remarkably study of insanity. Five beautiful, but demented, girls, all dressed alike and said by the custodian to be sisters, are depicted a prey to various forms of mania. One gazes terrified into space, another heavenward in ecstasy, a third clutches a love token, a fourth a rosary, while the fifth sits apart absorbed in gloomy imaginings. A nun in the background presides over the sad scene. A Madonna and Child by Antonio Saliba da Messina, dated 1497, also attributed to his master the great Antonello, and a powerful St. Christopher by Pietro Novelli, are the most important among the Old Masters.

Catania has for centuries been considered the literary metropolis of Sicily, and since Alphonso of Aragon

An Enjoyable Excursion

founded the University in 1444 it has been the chief seat of learning in the island. It has produced many famous men, earliest among them being Anphinomus and Anapia, *Pii Fratres*, who, in the eruption of 121 B.C., saved their parents by carrying them on their shoulders across the lava stream, which opened to let them pass. They were favourite heroes with the Latin poets and were represented on the coins of the city.

More recent celebrities are the novelist Giovanni Verga, the dramatist Luigi Capuana, the poet Mario Rapisardi and the actors Giovanni Grasso and Angelo Musco, besides the great composer Vincenzo Bellini, Catania's most famous son, to whose memory a fine statue by Monteverde stands in the Piazza Stesicoro. His house in the Via Vittorio Emanuele has been arranged as a museum containing relics of the master.

Catania is now a prosperous commerical city and port, with a flourishing export trade in sulphur, oranges and lemons.

We must not leave Catania without a visit to the spacious Giardino Bellini whence a magnificent view of Etna may be enjoyed, especially at sunset, and the *Opira di Pupi*, that typical Sicilian entertainment which has been described in another chapter.

An enjoyable excursion by tram is to Aci Castello and Aci Trezza ; the latter is close to the extraordinary Scogli dei Ciclopi, a series of pointed basaltic rocks, very interesting geologically and said to be the missiles flung by blind Polyphemus at his escaping enemy, Odysseus. On the way we pass Ognina or Porto Ulisse, pointed out as the spot where the hero landed for his memorable adventure with the Cyclops. Aci Trezza, though only a fishing village, possesses quite a good restaurant with terrace overlooking the rocks ; it is much frequented

Round Etna

on summer evenings by the Catanese. Further on is Aci Reale, a watering place whose Thermal Establishment is on the site of the old Roman Baths. Aci Castello is another fishing village with a ruined castle crowning a high volcanic rock. Here Ruggero di Lauria defended himself in 1297 against Frederick II. Flowers sprout among the crevices and luxuriate in the small neglected garden ; from the ruined tower the view of rocks and sea is very fine.

These places all take their name from Acis, the lover of the nymph Galatea and another victim of the jealousy of Polyphemus, who, while still in possession of his single eye, crushed his rival with a well-aimed rock, but the nymph changed him into a river which disappears underground in this neighbourhood. " Reale " was added by Philip V out of gratitude for the loyal succour accorded him by the small town.

Catania is the best starting-point for the ascent of Etna, a wonderful but fatiguing expedition which should not be undertaken before May or June. An interesting description of an ascent made in 1770 by Patrick Brydone will be found in his *Letters from Sicily to William Beckford*. It is somewhat easier now than in his day, for climbers can go as far as Nicholosi by motor-car, though from there they must proceed on mules or on foot.

If we cannot climb to great Mongibello's snowy summit and look down into the vast crater, the next best thing is to travel round the mountain and thus form some idea of its size and powers of destruction. The trip can be performed by train or motor-car, the latter occupying three or four hours from Catania to Taormina.

Passing through the towns of Misterbianco, Paternò, Biancavilla, Adernò, all of which have something interesting in their neighbourhood—mud springs, grottos

THE CLOISTERS OF SAN DOMENICO, TAORMINA

This famous monastery is now a fashionable hotel, but preserves many of its monastic characteristics,
notably a number of small cell-like bedrooms and these fascinating cloisters.

Picturesque Randazzo

and other volcanic phenomena—we come to Bronte, a sombre-looking town built of lava, formerly a haunt of brigands.

Between Bronte and Randazzo, at some distance from the main road, is the Castle of Maniace, once a Benedictine monastery, some of whose walls date from A.D. 1000, where in 1040 the Greek general, Maniaces, aided by a Norwegian army, defeated the Saracens. The castle is now the property of Sir Alexander Nelson Hood, K.G., Duke of Bronte, a descendant of Nelson, to whom the estates and title were given by Ferdinand IV of Naples, in recognition of his services. The chief value of this wild dukedom on the slopes of Etna lies in its extensive orange groves, which produce in great quantities a rare quality of fruit. The castle contains huge granaries for storing the corn with which the tenant farmers pay their rent. It has its own chapel and post office ; at sunset the gates are closed and savage dogs let loose to patrol the courtyard. In strange contrast with all this is the fine old English furniture within.

Randazzo is the most important town of the Etna circuit and the nearest to the crater ; hitherto the eruptions have always spared it. Very picturesque it is with its lava houses, ancient gateways and winding streets ; in common with Castrogiovanni it has been called the San Gimignano of Sicily.

The early origin of the town is shown by objects found in the neighbourhood. In the Middle Ages it was very important, and had the peculiarity of being inhabited by three separate populations speaking different dialects and having each its own bishop, who ruled the town for a term of three years each, the churches of Santa Maria, San Nicola and San Martino alternately serving as cathedral. For centuries the history of

Lava Fields

Randazzo was the history of these three churches with their squabbles and rivalry ; a rivalry which, no doubt, accounts for their richness in works of art. They all three contain good paintings and sculpture ; the architecture of the whole town is imposing.

In 1305 King Frederick of Aragon made Randazzo his summer residence, and the Aragon princes, his descendants, bore the title of Dukes of Randazzo.

Santa Maria was built early in the XIIIth century and possesses three apses and fine doors and windows. San Nicola was restored in 1582 but preserves something of its early aspect. Outside the church stands a curious statue representing the giant Pirammone. San Martino is of XVth and XVIIth-century architecture, but its magnificent *campanile*, in lava and limestone, with graceful windows, dates from the XIIIth century.

Beyond Randazzo the fertile valley of the Alcantara comes in sight, with Castiglione and Francavilla each on a frowning crag and the long chain of the Nebrodi Mountains stretching away to the north.

The road now passes through the lava zone of 1923. At one point it has been re-made at a level of several feet above the old road, which was completely destroyed, and passes between walls of piled-up lava, whose destructive force is here very evident. Near Linguaglossa two or three houses, all that are left of the village of Cerro, stand isolated with the lava piled high almost at their doors, the boiling stream having by an unaccountable freak flowed round them without overwhelming them.

Near this point are the celebrated " lava fields," a favourite excursion from Taormina. Here one can walk over the hot and smoking crust, which at a distance of several years from the eruption still shows no sign of cooling. It is like a scene from Dante's *Inferno ;* smoke

Taormina : its Charm

issues steadily from crevices in the surface, and a murky atmosphere, heavy with fumes like that of a covered railway station, broods over the black desolation of the scene. The great white cone, author of all this ruin, seems very near, and the dark streaks of the lava stream may be distinctly traced scarring its side.

The town of Linguaglossa was unharmed ; it possesses a Protector, Sant' Egidio, whose effigy was carried out to stem the fatal tide.

As we proceed downhill, passing through Piedimonte Etneo, we see the ancient lava stream which flowed to the sea and formed the rocks of Cape Schisò. The hill-tops are crowned by picturesque townlets or solitary watch-towers. We pass through groves of almonds, oranges and lemons to the sea, jolt along the rough main street of Giardini and up the many windings of the smoothly asphalted road, passing villas and luxuriant gardens, and so come to Taormina, that earthly paradise and goal of travellers, fairest flower of the Sicilian garden, favourite child of Etna, the great white mother.

To many persons the words Sicily and Taormina are synonymous, and to mention the one is to call up a vision of the other, for the little town nestling on its ledge high above the sea and sheltered by its background of mountains, is certainly the gem of the island.

Notwithstanding the cosmopolitan life of the place, in whose narrow Corso a jargon of tongues is heard and in whose luxurious hotels an ultra-fashionable crowd dances to the strains of the jazz band, Taormina, the real Taormina, preserves unspoiled its original character, its glowing romantic beauty. All through the mild winter roses and hibiscus are in bloom, oranges and lemons hang like fairy lamps amid the glossy foliage, while in January the first anemones and marigolds star

127

the grass and the asphodel rears on high its pale spikes of bloom. Soon the delicate almond blossom, light as a cloud of pink vapour, floats over the hill-sides and reflects great Etna's early morning blush.

Etna at dawn! Etna at sunrise! Etna at noon! Etna at sunset! Etna sleeping under the full moon! Who shall describe or compare the different phases of the glorious mountain, the presiding genius of Sicily and especially of Taormina? White against a salmon sky she awaits her lover the sun, her summit tipped with pink, like an immense almond flower; as he leaps up out of the sea she is wholly suffused with a rosy blush, then pales to primrose as the sky turns blue. All day she lies white under the sun's caress, her snowy bridal robe masking hidden fires. Again she blushes as he kisses her farewell and sinks out of sight, and in the afterglow her summit is outlined in living gold, fading once more to cold purity under the calm light of the full moon.

Taormina, in common with all Sicilian towns, has had an eventful history. It is believed to have been founded by the Siculians in the XIth century B.C., and to have had trading relations with the Phœnicians. In 306 B.C. it became the home of fugitives from Naxos or Schisò. Its definite history begins in 394, when Dionysius besieged it in vain, but returned in 392 and took it. In 345 the Siculian ruler Andromachus, father of the historian, Timæus, welcomed Timoleon's expedition. Later the town allied itself with the Carthaginians against Agathocles and afterwards with Rome. It became an important Byzantine centre, but curiously enough these rulers have left no trace.

For a long time Taormina resisted the Saracens, but at last fell under their power and traces of their domination

A SUNNY CORNER AT FORZA D'AGRO

All these good people were enjoying a sun-bath when Don Ciccio arrived with his grandchildren and
donkey and gladly posed for his portrait.

The Badia Vecchia

remain in walls and aqueducts. It is related that the aged Bishop Procopius was slain by the invaders and his heart devoured by the fierce Saracen chief Ibrahim-ibn-Ahmed.

In 1078 the Normans took possession of the city and all through the Middle Ages it was prosperous and important. In 1401 the Parliament of Barons met in the Palazzo Corvaia to elect a King of Sicily. The French took both Taormina and Mola in 1676, but in the following year a party of soldiers hoisted themselves by ropes up the cliff of Mola and surprised the French garrison. Taormina was occupied by General Filangieri in 1849. In 1860 Garibaldi, on board the ship *Franklin*, sailed from Giardini to continue his victorious progress on the mainland.

The Greek city was probably in the eastern part of the present town, as most of the classical remains lie in that direction, while the mediæval buildings, with the exception of Palazzo Corvaia, are chiefly to the west of the clock tower, said to be of Siculian origin, from which the ancient wall of circuit extends up the hill, cutting the town in half.

The Porta Catania bears the arms of Aragon, the seven towers of the city and the date 1440. Beyond this is another gateway, Porta Sant' Antonio, and a second protecting wall, as this side was more exposed to attack. Between the two walls is the small church of Sant' Antonio.

A conspicuous object on the hill-side is the tower of the Badia Vecchia with its three beautiful XVth-century windows; it is a favourite subject with artists when the surrounding almond trees are in flower. The Palazzo Santo Stefano is somewhat in the same style and both have the effective black and white decoration, carried

The Pride of Taormina

out in lava and limestone, which we see on many buildings in Taormina.

The present town consists mainly of the Corso Umberto, a long, narrow street flanked by uneven, picturesque buildings of various epochs and extending from one gate to the other. All the chief shops are in this street and it is the most frequented promenade, where visitors and residents meet many times in the day. Numbers of ancient doorways open on attractive courtyards and from the railings of the Piazza the ground falls away precipitously to the sparkling sea far below.

The churches, although externally picturesque, contain little of interest, except San Domenico, which has some good carving, a graceful marble Madonna and a tomb with a recumbent warrior, one of the Corvaia family.

In the Varò church is a painting by Antonio Giuffrè, who is said to have been the great Antonello's master.

The fountain in the Piazza del Duomo is surmounted by the emblem of Taormina, a strange monster, half human half bull, perhaps the Minotaur, whose name seems to be in some way connected with the town.

Near the Porta Messina is the fine Gothic Palazzo Corvaia, now ruined, with some beautiful windows and a curious relief on the staircase of Adam digging and Eve spinning. Close by are the remains of a small Roman theatre or Odeum and many fragments of ancient walls and arches.

Turning to the right we come to the splendid Greek Theatre, the pride of Taormina and too well known to need description. It is the largest in Sicily after that of Syracuse, and the stage, which was built by the Romans on the Greek foundation, is well preserved and shows a number of columns and arches. Through the wide

Church of San Pancrazio

opening snowy Etna is seen, with the deeply indented coastline and intensely blue sea. The theatre is red, being chiefly built of Roman brick, and the colour effect against the green hill-side is indescribably beautiful, as is the view on all sides, for it stands on a high promontory.

For the lover of country walks, long or short, Taormina is a paradise indeed. Among the longer outings, though quite within the capacity of an average walker, is Monte Venere (2834 feet), from whose summit there is a wonderful view. Monte Ziretto is nearer and easier of access. In the same direction but only just outside the Messina Gate, an ancient aqueduct spans a narrow gorge, in which is the garden once belonging to the writer, Robert Hichens, some of whose best work was done in the summer house he built there.

From the Catania Gate a path leads down to Giardini on the shore, whence one can proceed to Cape Schisò, whose black lava rocks stretch out to sea and are reached through luxuriant lemon groves. This was the ancient Naxos, the first landing-place of the Greeks in Sicily.

Above the town is the Castello di Taormina, a Norman ruin on the site of the ancient Acropolis. Somewhat further and higher is the hill town of Mola, which can now be reached by a good road. From these two heights with their magnificent panorama it is easy to realise how impregnable Taormina was in the past. In the church of Mola there is a curious wooden statue of St. George, the Protector of the town. The few ruins of the castle stand on a pinnacle of rock.

Close to the Messina Gate is the church of San Pancrazio, a disciple of St. Peter and the Patron of Taormina ; it is on the site of a temple of Jupiter Serapis and Apollo Archagetes. In a niche above the High Altar a curious XVth-century wooden statue of the Saint in episcopal

Round about Taormina

robes sits in a gilded palanquin, ready to be carried in procession at his *festa* in July. His face and hands are of a warm chocolate brown. Outside the church the wide arches of a ruined cloister frame exquisite glimpses of blue sea and almond blossom.

A steep, winding path leads down to the shore, to Isola Bella, a picturesque overgrown rock reached by a narrow isthmus of white sand. On the one hand the grotesque pointed rocks of the Capo di Taormina jut out into the sea ; on the other rises the solid headland of Capo Sant' Andrea, honeycombed with wonderful caves. Where the path joins the main road, opposite Isola Bella, a small, unpretentious wine shop bears this legend :

> Al sole che splende
> Buon vino si vende !
> Venite pronti
> Pria che tramonti !
>
> (Where bright shines the sun
> Good wine we supply !
> Come hasten to buy
> Ere daylight be done !)

In a Trattoria close by, whose terrace faces the sunny bay of Mazzerò, an excellent meal of fresh fish may be enjoyed at a modest price. The Bathing Establishments of Isola Bella and Mazzerò are both provided with restaurant and pension.

Beyond the Capo di Mazzerò an islet joined to the cliff by a curious causeway is the scene of the tragedy in Hichens' *Call of the Blood*.

About two miles further along the coast is the village of Letoyanni, famous for its February Fair, when a wide, dry river-bed becomes a temporary cattle market, and swarms with peasants and their animals.

Photo   *Audigier*

THE CLOCK TOWER, TAORMINA

This quaint tower, said to be of Sicilian origin, divides the town in half,
the classic remains being on one side, and the mediæval on the other.

Forza d'Agro

Beyond this we see the bold headland of Sant' Alessio, crowned by an ancient castle. Stretching along the ridge above is the Norman town of Forza d' Agrò, which is well worth a visit. A zigzag road whose sharp corners require careful driving, leads up to the uneven Piazza, facing which is the church of Sant' Agostino with a XVth-century door. This church contains two valuable works of art : a fine painting by Antonello da Messina, Abraham and the three Angels, and the ancient *gonfalone* of the Confraternity, a heavy frame of richly carved and gilded wood whose two faces bear inset the Madonna and Child and Abraham with the three Angels. These *gonfaloni* are extremely rare in Sicily, as they fell into disuse early in the XVIIth century, when the Spaniards introduced the standards still in use in processions.

The cathedral is an XVIIIth-century structure added to the XIVth-century church ; the *campanile* is of the earlier date. The church contains carved choir stalls, a good Annunciation of the school of Antonello and a curious XIVth-century painted crucifix.

Another small church has a XVIth-century statue of St. Catherine by Montanini.

The chief attraction of Forza d' Agrò is the view from the ruined castle, to which we climb by steep and dirty *vicoli*. It was built by Count Roger and restored in the XVth century ; the tower of Roger's church within the walls is still standing. The castle enclosure has for many years been used as a cemetery, and owing to the impossibility of digging down into the rock, most of the tombs are formed of large blocks of cement. It is a somewhat inaccessible burying-place ; the bearers have to stagger with the weight of the coffin on their shoulders up the slippery path, which provides a precarious foothold even for those who are unencumbered !

Savoca

On another hill-top at some distance is the fascinating town of Savoca, with the remains of a Saracen castle and some beautiful XVth-century doorways. Savoca was formerly celebrated for the bravery of its inhabitants and the goodness of its wine ; perhaps the one accounts for the other !

But these are only two of the many picturesque townlets scattered over the hills between Messina and Taormina. Here, as in the interior of Sicily, there is scarcely a town or village which does not repay a visit. Unfortunately many of these places are difficult of access and devoid of accommodation, but the traveller who can brave a little discomfort is always richly rewarded.

No account of Taormina is complete without mention of Giovanni, the one-legged flute player. For many years—how many it would be difficult to say—he has been a familiar figure near the Greek Theatre or on the stone seat overlooking the ravine outside the Catania Gate, and the full-throated, birdlike notes of his primitive flute have added to the bucolic charm of the scene.

No one can render so well as Giovanni the haunting melody of the *Pastorale*—that tune played for centuries by the mountain shepherds when at Christmas they come trooping down with music to pay their homage to the newborn Christ. No one like Giovanni can give that mad, swinging rhythm to the *tarantella*, which compels even unaccustomed feet to dance ! And few even in pagan Taormina have that intense, faun-like joy of living which surrounds him like an aura, lame though he is and far from young !

On my last visit to Taormina I heard near the Greek Theatre a feeble tootling which emphatically was *not* Giovanni, and came upon a piper with two legs and no

AT THE CONVENT PORTAL

No applicant is ever turned away by the good nuns, who provide soup for
the old and schooling for the young.

The Pastorale

crutch sitting in Giovanni's accustomed place. With a tightening at the heart I asked for news of my old friend and heard with relief that he was not dead, only gone away, though that was bad enough. But on approaching the Catania Gate later in the day, the triumphant notes of the *Pastorale* played with consummate skill reached my ears ; and there on the stone seat sat Giovanni, piping vigorously and nodding in time to his music. He welcomed me with a radiant smile.

" Oh, Giovanni," I cried, seizing his hand, " so you have not gone away ! The other piper told me. . . . But how badly he plays ! "

" Cosa vuole, gli manca l' arte ! " (What would you, he has no art !) he replied, thus indulgently disposing of his would-be rival, and added, summing up this and every circumstance of life with his usual formula :

" Basta che ci sia la salute ! " (To have good health is enough !)

Dear, cheerful old Giovanni, long may his music, gay and pagan, proclaim the doctrine of eternal youth amid the almond blossom of Taormina !

CHAPTER X

A RUN of three hours from Taormina brings us, through some of the finest scenery in Sicily, to Tindari, an outpost of Greek civilisation on the north coast and one of the most beautiful spots in the island.

The traveller with only a day or so at his disposal will do well to pay at least a hurried visit to this fascinating place ; but more fortunate is he who can spend a week dreaming in the garden of the Grand Hotel, watching the changing colours of sea and mountain at sunrise and sunset, and visiting the interesting ruins whose partial excavation lends an added charm of mystery, for we feel sure that the grass and flowers conceal greater treasures than any they have already yielded.

The road from Taormina follows the Alcantara Valley as far as Francavilla, then turns sharply to the right and begins climbing up into the heart of the Peloritan Mountains. The luxuriant vegetation of valleys and foothills is exchanged for the gloomy majesty of pine-woods ; the air grows keen, even cold, and the circle of mountains crowned by Etna is shut out from view by the chilly mist. At length we reach the crest of the pass, emerge from the mist and descend through acres of golden broom to Novara, on the slope of Rocca Novara, the highest peak of the Peloritan range. We now descend rapidly to sea-level, cross a bridge of seventeen arches which spans the *fiumare* or dry river-bed of the

The Theatre

Mazzarrà or Vigliatore (the ancient Helicon) and ascend the winding road that leads to Tindari.

The pointed headland crowned by a white church and group of buildings is a remarkable feature in the landscape and the goal of many a pilgrimage, for the Black Madonna of Tindari enjoys world-wide fame, and her cult supplanted that of the Heavenly Twins, Castor and Pollux, the Tyndarides, who had their sanctuary on the same spot and gave their name to the town. They were the protectors of sailors and therefore of the sailor-colonists from Messina and Locri, with whom Dionysius peopled the territory of Abacænum, now Tripi—one of the last colonies founded in 396 B.C.

Tindari soon became a flourishing centre of maritime commerce and possessed, besides the Temple of Castor and Pollux, one to Demeter, who gave the rich harvests of the fertile land, and one to Hermes, patron of traders. In this temple stood the famous golden statue of Hermes which was stolen by the Carthaginians, restored by Scipio Africanus and again carried off by Verres, thus providing Cicero with the theme for one of his finest orations.

The engineers and builders sent by Dionysius, the same probably who had built the Castle of Euryalus at Syracuse, soon surrounded the new city with a double circuit of walls, so marvellously constructed that their remains are considered the finest example of Greek walls in existence.

The theatre was built in the reign of Timoleon and could seat 3000 spectators. It occupied a splendid position on the highest point of the promontory with a view of the sea and Æolian Islands. Although to the uninitiated it appears more ruined than the other Greek theatres in Sicily, archæologists declare it to

Story of the Madonna

be the only one which gives a true idea of the Greek stage.

The remains of a large building evidently Roman bear the name Gymnasium, though it is uncertain what purpose it served. Close by are two rooms with mosaic pavement and traces of frescoes on the walls. Several Roman statues and busts found at Tindari are now in the Museum at Palermo.

Under the Romans the prosperity of Tindari declined and a landslide in A.D. 19 precipitated part of the city into the sea, blocking up the fine harbour.

Tindari embraced Christianity in the IInd century and it is probable that an early church was built on the site of the Temple of Castor and Pollux, being rebuilt and enlarged in the XVIth century.

The city was occupied and partially destroyed by the Saracens in 836.

The façade of the church has a curiously small door surrounded by allegorical bas-reliefs. The interior is very plain, even the altar of the Black Madonna having none of the rich decoration usual in such shrines. Yet this Madonna is considered miraculous and on the 8th of September every year thousands of pilgrims flock to pay her homage.

Legend relates that the statue was brought in remote times on a ship from some unknown place. A storm drove the vessel into the small bay which was all that remained of the once famous harbour of Tyndaris; when it had abated and the sailors wished to resume their voyage, the ship refused to move. All efforts with oars and sails were unavailing; as a last hope they unloaded the cargo, and no sooner was the statue carried on shore than wind filled the sails and the ship proceeded swiftly on her way. The Madonna's desire to remain in that

Photo   *Cutler*

ON THE ROAD TO MOLA

These peasants are bringing their chickens and young goats down from
their mountain villages to sell in Taormina. Mola on the hill was once an
impregnable stronghold.

A Local Piper

spot was evident, and she was carried up the hill and placed in the modest church, in the second chapel on the right, where she still is. Later it was thought more seemly to place her on the High Altar, but here again she showed her decided preference for her original resting-place, returning to it three times unaided, until the monks were persuaded to leave her there in peace !

The Madonna is carved in black wood and holds the Child on her knee. On the base of the statue is inscribed the verse from the Song of Solomon : " Nigra sum sed formosa " (I am black but comely). The statue is obviously of Byzantine origin and its dark complexion forms no obstacle to the fervent devotion with which it is regarded.

The charm of Tindari is felt by all who visit it. King Edward VII, when there in 1907, said : " It is a veritable corner of paradise ! " In natural beauty it is not inferior to Taormina, while for the dreamer and lover of solitude it is an abode of peace where as yet the fashionable crowd has not penetrated. Formerly there was no good accommodation, but about 1926 the Grand Hotel was opened by an amateur archæologist possessing the appropriate name of Giuseppe Pace. Happening to visit Tindari in search of ancient coins, he became enamoured of the place, bought the only good-sized villa with a garden and a glorious view, and turned it into a hotel, for which all travellers who have felt the charm of Tindari owe him a debt of gratitude.

During dinner the local shepherd piper plays the *cornamusa*, and the weird strains, similar to those of the Scottish bagpipes, ring out strangely on the still evening air. This man in his sheepskin cap and leggings may be seen at sunset leaning against a wall and playing a small flute to call his sheep home to the fold. At the sound of one particular tune they hasten to his side, obedient as dogs, but are apparently deaf to all the other tunes in his repertoire!

The most convenient station for Tindari is Patti, although Oliveri is somewhat nearer. The small town of Patti boasts a cathedral built by Count Roger, who founded two monasteries there. His widow Adelasia, after her wise regency and her unhappy second marriage with Baldwin, King of Jerusalem, brother of Godfrey de Bouillon, returned to Sicily and spent her last years in works of charity. She lived at Patti in the castle built by Saracen architects for her son King Roger, and was buried in a magnificent marble sarcophagus in the cathedral.

As we read her Latin epitaph we think how strange it is that this famous princess, whose dowry enabled the Great Count to deliver Sicily from the Saracens and who ruled the new kingdom so wisely during the minority of its first king, afterwards becoming Queen of Jerusalem, should come to her last rest in the obscure town of Patti, noted only for the manufacture of earthenware household utensils!

Sic transit gloria mundi!

From the height of Tindari we enjoy a fine view of the Æolian Islands, a volcanic group aptly described by Guy de Maupassant as "fantastic flowers of sulphur blossoming in the midst of the sea." On a clear day Etna may be seen smoking on the one hand, Stromboli far away on the other, while the twin peaks of Salina and the cone of Vulcano look as though at any moment they might burst into flames. These attractive islets, notwithstanding their nearness to the coast, are almost unknown to tourists, for accommodation is scanty, Lipari being the only one which possesses a tolerable

A FOUNTAIN AT MESSINA

In this elaborate fountain by Michelangelo's pupil Montorsoli, Orion stands
on a high column supported by allegorical figures, while four river gods
recline below.

Lipari

hotel. Steamers ply from Milazzo, but the boats are so small that in bad weather they often cannot cross the narrow channel, which is swept by all the winds of heaven, just as it was in the days of Odysseus, when King Æolus entrusted him with the bag of winds and his sailors imprudently allowed them to escape!

Once safely arrived at Lipari there is much to see, and excursions can be made to the other islets, Vulcano and Salina being the most interesting; a longer trip takes us to Stromboli, that restless, ever-active volcano.

Geologically these islands are very interesting; they were formed under the sea and began to emerge in the tertiary period. Lipari is exceedingly fertile and produces excellent wine, its Malvasia being largely exported. It possesses a number of spent craters, hot springs and other volcanic phenomena, the most remarkable being the beds of pumice stone and streams of obsidian, a vitreous volcanic product used by the prehistoric inhabitants for arms and utensils. These streams have somewhat the appearance of glaciers, while the sulphur cascades are like crystallised sunshine; in the rich soil prickly pear, broom and caper grow to gigantic proportions. Everything in the island seems fantastic and unreal, like the landscape in a dream.

In 578 B.C. a Greek colony was founded at Lipari; later it was allied with Syracuse and was attacked by the Athenians in 427 B.C. and by the Carthaginians in 397. Agathocles plundered the temples in 301. During the Punic Wars it was a Carthaginian naval base; the Romans took it in 252 and Sextus Pompeius used it for the same purpose. The Romans exploited the thermal springs of the island and later sent political exiles there. In more recent times it was a convict station, and a large part of the present quiet, orderly population are the

A Gruesome Discovery

descendants of convicts and exiles, so that all the dialects of Italy are spoken in the small town.

Vulcano possesses three craters, one of which was in eruption a few years ago. The two craters of Salina are spent, but curious eruptive phenomena take place occasionally under the sea near the coast, causing great mortality among fish; on these occasions there is a strong odour of sulphur in the air.

Fishing is the staple industry of all these islands, and Stromboli produces good wine.

Milazzo, the ancient Mylæ, was founded in 716 B.C. by Greeks from Messina, and possesses a sheltered harbour where in 260 B.C. the Roman Consul Duilius won a great naval victory over the Carthaginians. In July 1860 a decisive battle was fought here by Garibaldi against the Bourbon troops under General Bosco, who took refuge in the castle and was forced to capitulate. This castle is the only object of interest in the sleepy little town. Built in the XIIIth century it was added to by Charles V and restored in the XVIIth century. It was besieged several times in the Spanish wars. It stands on a rocky platform commanding the town and the sea on both sides of a narrow isthmus, and the view from the keep is magnificent, with the long line of the Peloritan Mountains terminating in Cape Rasocolmo, the northernmost point of Sicily, on the right, and the Æolian Islands temptingly near.

In February, 1928, a gruesome discovery was made at the Castle of Milazzo. In the new fervour for the cultivation of every available bit of ground, a party of convicts (the castle is now used as a prison), were set to dig a patch of virgin soil close under the walls. Legends of buried treasure are rife here as in all mediæval castles, so when the spades struck against something hard and metallic the men redoubled their efforts, expecting to bring to light an iron-bound chest full of gold coins.

What were their surprise and horror on finding that their *treasure-trove* was a large iron cage containing a human skeleton minus hands and feet ! Examination showed it to be the skeleton of a young man of more than average height, and some regimental buttons found near it bore the word " Enniskillen " and the number 27.

Evidently the victim of this diabolical instrument of torture belonged to the famous Irish regiment. But how came he to Milazzo Castle and why was he condemned to a horrible, lingering death, aggravated perhaps by mutilation ? The cage was so constructed as to press the arms to the sides and hold the legs apart. It was provided with a ring to suspend it by and had two sharp spikes worked by screws to pierce the victim's neck.

Did this evil instrument belong to the Inquisition which once had its Office adjoining the church within the castle walls ? For some reason the body was hastily buried, cage and all, in a shallow grave, and with it was buried the secret of the unhappy Irishman's name and history.

. . . .

Our Sicilian tour is drawing to a close, and it is fitting that it should end with Messina, the nearest point to Italy, and the last place from which the Bourbons were expelled ; Messina, the brave but unfortunate city, which seems singled out by the forces of Nature for destruction, but which like the phœnix ever rises again from its own ashes, to new and intenser life.

The history of Messina is one long tale of tenacity and courage, and of the patient, undying love of the Sicilians for their native soil.

History

According to Hesiod the city was founded by no less a personage than Orion, the Mighty Hunter, while Kronos or Saturn, dropping his reaping hook there, formed the curving harbour and gave it its early name, Zancle. Poseidon, lord of the ocean and friend of mariners, was its tutelary deity and many temples were raised in his honour; but the Earthshaker proved faithless to his trusting worshippers and the city has suffered severely from earthquakes and tidal waves.

Zancle was first a Siculian city; it was captured by Cumæan pirates and colonised by the Chalcidians about 730 B.C. About 493 it was taken by fugitives from Samos and Miletus, then by Anaxilas of Reggio, who changed its name to Messana in memory of Messene, his place of origin. Later the city allied itself alternately with Akragas and Syracuse, being taken by the Athenians in 426. It was conquered and destroyed by the Carthaginians under Himilcon in 396 B.C., but restored by Dionysius and again by Timoleon. In 288 B.C. the Mamertines, expelled from Sicily after the death of Agathocles, Tyrant of Syracuse, were hospitably received at Messina and possessed themselves by treachery of the city. They repulsed the attacks of Pyrrhus but could not hold out against Hiero of Syracuse, and in 269 they appealed to Rome for help, which brought the Romans to Sicily and caused the First Punic War.

Messina flourished under Roman and Byzantine dominion, also under the Saracens, who gained possession of it in A.D. 831. The Normans came in 1061, and the city became, from its position, an important commercial emporium during the Crusades. It suffered at the hands of Richard Cœur de Lion and his unruly followers in 1190.

The city was unsuccessfully besieged by Charles of Anjou in 1282, and made a heroic resistance, in which

CAPO SANT' ANDREA, TAORMINA

This headland with its wonderful caves and rocks divides the Bay of
Taormina from that of Mazzero, and is a favourite spot for picnics.

History

the women took part. Charles V visited it in 1535 and bestowed upon it many privileges ; Don John of Austria the victor of Lepanto, was welcomed there in 1571.

In 1674 the Spaniards were driven out and Louis XIV of France, whose help had been sought by the Messinese, hoped to establish his dominion in the island ; but he was obliged to withdraw his ships and Messina was severely punished by the returning Spaniards, who built a strong fortress overlooking the city.

In the XVIIIth century two great misfortunes befell Messina ; about 40,000 inhabitants died of plague in 1743, while in 1783 a terrible earthquake destroyed the greater part of the city.

Under the Bourbon tyranny there were repeated insurrections, and a bombardment in 1848, which compelled the brave city to capitulate, earned for Ferdinand II the nickname of King Bomba.

Messina was the last Italian city to reap the benefits of freedom, for though Garibaldi had entered in triumph in July 1860, it was only in March 1861 that she was finally able to join United Italy.

But the troubles of the devoted city were not yet over. An outbreak of cholera in 1854 carried off 15,000 inhabitants, an earthquake in 1894 did serious damage, and in December 1908 came the terrible disaster which nearly wiped Messina off the face of the globe.

Before her overthrow Messina was one of the most beautiful cities of Sicily. Backed by an amphitheatre of glorious mountains, the entire space between them and the sea was filled with fine palaces, wide streets and historic churches. The *palazzata* or sea front was renowned for its long line of symmetrical buildings reflected in the blue water, while across the glittering Strait the eye rested on the misty purple hills of Calabria.

The New Town

Hills, mountains and sea are still there in glowing beauty; but where is Messina—the prosperous Messina of the past? Gone, vanished; the dust of her palaces mingled with that of her dead population, 84,000 of them buried under the ruins of their homes.

The disaster happened at 5.20 a.m. on December 28th, 1908, when a shock of thirty seconds' duration razed to the ground practically the whole city. Many of the inhabitants passed from sleep to death; others endured untold horrors, pinned under fallen masonry from which they were only liberated after days and nights of torture. Many became hopelessly mad. Numerous other shocks succeeded the first and a huge tidal wave completed the devastation. The epicentrum was in the Strait itself between Messina and Reggio.

For several years Messina was nothing but a vast field of ruins, on whose outskirts a town of wooden huts grew up to shelter those survivors who refused to leave the neighbourhood of their ruined homes. But the Messinese were not daunted even by this tremendous disaster; patiently, silently, they began rebuilding their beloved city; an inscription on a house in the Viale San Martino records that the work of restoration began there, on January 5th, 1909, eight days after the disaster! What a testimonial to Sicilian tenacity and courage!

A new city has now arisen, carefully planned, with wide streets, spacious squares and handsome, though low-pitched, public buildings. Armoured cement and anti-seismic iron frames are used and no building, public or private, is allowed to exceed two storeys in height. A few streets on the edge of the danger zone have still their original high houses standing on the one side, while on the other everything is new and uniform.

Works of Art

Interesting and admirable though all this is, a visit to Messina need not occupy many hours, for alas, few historic monuments are left. Of these the most important is the cathedral or Matrice, built by Count Roger in 1092 on the site of a IVth or VIth-century church. Fire, earthquake and restoration had already made it a strange mixture of styles when it was almost entirely overthrown in 1908 ; only the apse, the façade and a small portion of wall were left standing ; the façade was partially demolished for safety and is being rebuilt. A fine Gothic door with marble ornamentation is intact. Of the twenty-six granite columns in the interior, said to have come from a temple of Poseidon at the Faro, only three are left, and in their fall a magnificent XIIIth-century ceiling was lost. The High Altar and rich mosaics of the choir escaped injury, as did also the inlaid XVIth-century choir stalls.

The church of the Santissima Annunziata dei Catalani, the earliest Norman church in Messina, built in the late XIIth century on the site of a temple and perhaps of a mosque, was not badly damaged and is architecturally interesting.

The other churches are being restored wherever possible, but one whose loss is greatly regretted is San Gregorio, on whose terrace Goethe is said to have written his immortal poem, " Kennst Du dass Land ? " Certainly the view from that spot and the perfume of its lemon groves are calculated to inspire a poet's divinest flights.

In the Museum we find all that has been saved from the wreck of churches and palaces ; of special note is the *Polittico*, Antonello da Messina's masterpiece, and a statue by Gagini.

Two magnificent works of art which fortunately

The Vara

escaped destruction are the fountains by Montorsoli. That of Orion stands in the Piazza del Duomo ; that of Poseidon near the harbour is now replaced by an excellent copy by the local sculptor Zappalà, the original being preserved in the Museum.

These two colossal fountains were erected in the XVIth century to celebrate the bringing to Messina of the Camaro water. They are masterpieces of sculpture. In the one the Sea God stands with his back to the Strait and with outstretched arm quells the fury of Scylla and Charybdis, represented as double-tailed sirens with malignant faces. In the other Orion stands on a high column supported by graceful nymphs and allegorical figures, while round the wide basin recline statues representing the rivers Nile, Tiber, Ebro and Camaro.

The Festival of the Assumption (August 15th) is a great day at Messina. For centuries the Vara, an immense pyramidal car covered with figures of saints and angels with Christ at the summit holding Madonna's soul in his hand, was taken in procession through the streets. Two gigantic equestrian figures also paraded the city on this festival, and were called in different epochs " King Zancleo and his Queen," or " Mata and Grifone." The man was black and the woman white ; they were supposed to live in the castle of Matagrifone above Messina. They may have symbolised the Normans and Saracens or the position of Sicily between Europe and Africa.

These remarkable figures were reduced to fragments in the earthquake, but have now been restored, together with the Vara, and the traditional procession has been revived. At one time groups of living figures stood on the Vara, the Madonna being represented by a young girl who had the privilege of obtaining pardon for a condemned criminal.

No one should leave Messina without paying a visit to the Camposanto, or cemetery, which is one of the most beautiful spots in the city, a cool green oasis amid the dust of building and restoration. On entering its gates we find ourselves in a luxuriant southern garden ; the few tombs in sight are half-hidden by drooping foliage ; a wide expanse of artistic carpet bedding slopes up to the central building, the domed mausoleum of Giuseppe La Farina and other patriots. Higher still the Gothic spire of a chapel appears above the trees. Shady, flower bordered paths lead right and left to the chapels and monuments, mostly modern but in good taste. One which brings tears to the eyes was erected by the coast-guards in memory of their comrades who perished in the disaster of 1908. Under a mass of overhanging rock lie several nude figures, dead or dying ; one of their number seems to be supporting the whole weight of the block on his arms and shoulders, holding it back from his companions. A comrade in the uniform of the Guardie di Finanza stands gazing sorrowfully at the group. The monument bears one of those touching inscriptions which Italians know so well how to write.

Not far from Messina, in a valley of lemon groves, is one of the earliest Norman churches in Sicily : Santa Maria di Mili, built by Count Roger in 1082 for the Basilian monks.

This tiny church is architecturally interesting, showing as it does the model on which a whole series of early Norman churches in Eastern Sicily was built. Its three small domes recall San Giovanni degli Eremiti in Palermo, and though somewhat spoilt by early restoration, the church still preserves its ancient form and picturesqueness.

In 1092 Jourdain, Roger's brave son who took part in the conquest of Trapani and fell fighting against the Saracens of Pantalica, was buried in the sacristy of Santa Maria di Mili, as an inscription records, after solemn funeral ceremonies at Syracuse.

An interesting drive along the coast from Messina brings us to the Faro, near Cape Peloro at the narrowest part of the Strait, which is here less than three miles wide. Opposite is Scylla, the rock which, according to Homer and Virgil, was the home of a terrible many-headed monster which devoured those mariners who escaped the clutches of Charybdis, another monster whose lair was under Cape Peloro, and which swallowed the waters of the sea thrice daily and threw them up again. There is to this day a perilous whirlpool called Garofalo at this point, and the strong currents make navigation dangerous.

Off the Faro a number of large fishing boats may be observed, each carrying an abnormally high mast. These are for the capture of the swordfish, an important industry of Messina and an exciting sport. Perched on high in a kind of crow's-nest, a lynx-eyed fisherman surveys the sea, and when the coveted fish appears he gives the signal to an attendant light skiff, which skims swiftly over the surface and captures the quarry. This look-out man remains for hours at his post, even under the burning sun, his head protected by a wide-brimmed hat.

The Messinese are wonderful swimmers and divers and uphold the tradition of the famous Cola Pesce, immortalised by Schiller in *Der Taucher*. This marvellous diver feared not the insidious currents and eddies of the Straits, and one day he brought back from the depths of the

Fata Morgana

dreaded Garofalo whirlpool a golden cup flung by King Frederick. Again the King flung the cup and again Cola Pesce plunged in unhesitatingly. But this time the spirits of the deep claimed their prey; the boiling waters surged up once more, but the heroic diver was no more seen.

Another and earlier legend of the Straits has been resuscitated by Morselli in his exquisite dramatic poem *Glaucus*. It is the story of a Sicilian fisher-lad torn by two rival passions—desire for glory and love for the gentle Scilla, whose father, a rich shepherd, refused to give her to the penniless youth, who was "too great a dreamer to be even a good fisherman."

Glaucus sailed away to join Jason's expedition, swearing to return a king and to make Scilla his queen. After many adventures he snatched from Circe the kiss of immortality, sprang on board his ship and hurried home to Sicily—only to find that his beloved Scilla had thrown herself into the sea in despair at his prolonged absence.

Cursing the immortality which prevented him from joining her in death, he caused himself to be chained living to the beloved corpse and flung into the sea. And his cries and laments still come booming up on stormy nights from the restless depths of the Strait. . . .

A curious phenomenon called Fata Morgana may be observed from Reggio on hot, calm days. The Sicilian coast seems to approach and buildings are reflected, magnified and distorted in the air or water, taking the form of fairy cities or hosts of armed men. It is similar to the mirage of the desert, and is not visible from the Sicilian side of the Straits, but seems to hang like a veil of mystery over Trinacria's magic land.

And now our wanderings in that land are over; it is

Fata Morgana

time to say farewell to Sicily, Island of the Sun, land of myth and beauty. At Messina we embark on the ferry-boat which carries a number of railway coaches securely on its broad deck and glides steadily and smoothly across the Strait, defying Scylla, Charybdis and all the monsters of the deep.

As the strip of water widens between us and the exquisite Messina coast, we reflect how the much-tried city with its sickle-shaped harbour and protecting mountains, has awakened to new life and activity—a fitting symbol of the New Italy, springing up on the foundations of ancient greatness and past misfortune, her eyes trustfully fixed on the rising sun of a glorious future.

Index

Index

Index

Index

Index

157

Studies in Modern Music

By Sir W. H. HADOW, M.A.

Volume I: BERLIOZ, SCHUMANN & WAGNER

With an Essay on Music & Musical Criticism
With Four Portraits

Eleventh Edition. 5s. nett each. Also a Library Edition
8s. 6d. nett

"One more bit of advice is necessary. READ NOW, IF YOU
HAVE NOT READ IT BEFORE, THE OPENING ESSAY
IN THE FIRST VOLUME OF SIR HENRY HADOW'S
'STUDIES IN MODERN MUSIC,' in which the main characteristics of beauty in music are clearly defined. Nothing could assist you
better in the task of 'arranging your emotions' and obtaining a glimpse of
the reasons experienced music-lovers have for describing works as beautiful
or the reverse."—Extract from *Musical Taste & How to Form It*, by
M. D. Calvocoressi.

"The first attempt towards laying the foundations of a specific method in
musical criticism is Hadow's (*Studies in Modern Music*, London, Seeley,
Service & Co., First Series), who disengages the four main principles—
vitality, labour, proportion and fitness—from the existence of which
estimates of musical works can be arrived at."—Extract from *The
Dictionary of Modern Music & Musicians.*

Volume II: CHOPIN, DVOŘÁK & BRAHMS

With an Essay on Musical Form. With Four Portraits

Eleventh Edition. Crown 8vo, 5s. nett. Also a Library
Edition, 8s. 6d. nett

"The development of form is described with many brilliant touches and
with complete grasp of the subject, and the book, which will probably be
considered to be EVEN BETTER THAN THE FORMER WORK,
is most heartily to be recommended to all who wish to attain the highest
kind of enjoyment of the best music."—*Times.*

CALENDAR FOR READERS

Where to go in the First half of the year

JANUARY. Black Forest (Winter Sports), **CEYLON**, China, **EGYPT**, India, Morocco (Coast Towns, e.g. Tangier), Riviera, **SWEDEN** (Winter Sports), **SWITZERLAND** (Winter Sports).

FEBRUARY. Black Forest (Winter Sports), **CEYLON**, China, **EGYPT**, India, Morocco (Coast Towns, e.g. Tangier), Naples, Palestine, Rome, **RIVIERA**, **SICILY**, **SOUTH SPAIN**, **SWEDEN** (Winter Sports), **Switzerland** (Winter Sports).

MARCH. Belgium, Ceylon, Egypt, India, Japan, **MOROCCO**, **NAPLES**, **PALESTINE**, **RIVIERA**, Rome, **SICILY**, North Spain, **CENTRAL and SOUTH SPAIN**.

APRIL. **BELGIUM**, Canary Islands, Channel Islands, Constantinople, Corsica, **FLORENCE**, **GREECE**, Holland, **ITALIAN LAKES**, **JAPAN**, **KASHMIR**, Madeira, **MOROCCO**, **NAPLES**, **PALESTINE**, **PARIS**, **PORTUGAL**, **PROVENCE**, **ROME**, Rhine, **RIVIERA**, **SHAKESPEARE'S COUNTRY**, **SICILY**, **NORTH CENTRAL and SOUTH SPAIN**, Switzerland, Venice, Vienna.

MAY. **BELGIUM**, Black Forest, **CAMBRIDGE**, Canary Islands, **CHANNEL ISLANDS**, Chateaux Country, **CONSTANTINOPLE**, Corsica, **DOLOMITES** (from middle of May), Edinburgh, English Lakes, **FLORENCE**, **GREECE**, Holland, **ITALIAN LAKES**, **KASHMIR**, London, Madeira, Morocco, Naples, **OXFORD**, **PARIS**, **PORTUGAL**, **PROVENCE**, Pyrenees, **RHINE** (from middle of May), Riviera, **ROME**, Shakespeare's Country, **SICILY**, **NORTH and CENTRAL SPAIN**, **SWITZERLAND**, Venice, Vienna, Wales.

JUNE. **BELGIUM**, Black Forest, Cambridge, Canada, **CHANNEL ISLANDS**, **CHATEAUX COUNTRY**, **CONSTANTINOPLE**, Corsica, **DOLOMITES**, **EDINBURGH**, Florence, **ENGLISH LAKES**, Holland, London, Normandy and Brittany, Norway, Oxford (first part of June) Paris, Portugal, **PYRENEES**, **RHINE**, **RUSSIA**, **SCOTTISH HIGHLANDS**, **NORTH SPAIN**, **SWEDEN**, Switzerland, Venice, Vienna.

FULLER particulars of When and Why to will be found in the volumes of the Service & Co. Ltd., London, under the title

The heavier type indicates the Months in